THE FIRE THAT BURNS WITHIN

RUFUS MONTGOMERY JR.

© 2022 by In The Mind Of Thomas
All rights reserved. No part of this publication may be reproduced, transmitted, or stored in an information retrieval system in any form or by any means, graphic, electronic, or mechanical, including photocopying, taping, and recording, without prior written permission from the author.

PUBLISHER'S NOTE
This is a work of fiction. Names, characters, places, and incidents either are the product of the author's imagination and experiences or are used fictitiously, and any resemblance to actual persons, living or dead, events, or locales is entirely coincidental.

Cover courtesy of INCO Designs

THE FIRE THAT BURNS WITHIN

1

MOVING THROUGH THE LIVING ROOM, I realize this is what it's all about. I'm wearing my best maroon suit and when I pass the gilded mirror, I pause a moment. Damn! I look good. I bring nothing with me but desire. I already know what room she sleeps in, and she is alone for the weekend. Passing by the coffee table, I smile at the possibilities. I see ribbons, candles, scissors, and a mostly empty bottle of wine. Possibilities ... indeed.

The house smells of potpourri and cookies, which would comfort most, but I find it annoying. It's thirty degrees outside, and the heat is off. Although this isn't my home, I've been here many times before. From the bottom of the stairs, I can hear her breathing slowly and peacefully. I walk up to the second floor, making my way to the master bedroom as my excitement builds.

RUFUS MONTGOMERY JR.

As I walk, feeling the plush carpet beneath my feet is too much for me.

The bedroom door ajar, I can smell her perfume and see inside. The moonlight beams through her window. There she lies. The blanket draped across her leaves her right shoulder and breast exposed. I savor the moment and take it all in, admiring the parts of her that I can see. It is time. I can wait no longer. Slowly pushing the door open, I smell the aroma of her skin. It is intoxicating. My chest rises as I breathe in her scent.

The sound of my gloves on the doorknob cuts the silence in the air like a knife. Entering the room with my eyes fixed on her bare breast—my lips moisten in anticipation of its taste.

I stand between her and the open window. I feel the cold on my back—the same cold that causes her nipple to be such a plump and pink vision. Grabbing a hand full of the covers, I slowly pull so not to wake her before the right time. The covers gently reveal her other breast and an equally arched left nipple. I stop to admire the sight of her naked body as a gust of wind fills the room. Slowly and softly, I crawl onto the bed.

RUFUS MONTGOMERY JR.

the look of confusion quickly followed by the look of fear. With my finger still firmly pushing in and out of her, I can feel her coming over and over as the life slowly leaves her body.

The smell of fear, pain, pleasure, and the sound of me inside her fill the room. It's almost more than I can take. Now that she has stopped moving, I go back downstairs. I remember the cookies. Maybe just one. Wouldn't want them to go to waste. As I put the last morsel in my mouth, a smile creeps across my face. She left me something. Now I'm left only with the taste of the sweetness left on my glove.

Oh, wait. You're probably wondering how we came to these delicious events, and why that beautiful woman had to die. Well, she didn't have to die—I just wanted her that way. And the way she died, God, if I could go back upstairs and do it all over ... I would do it again and again. Anyway, let me catch you up. I'll tell you how and why we came to this. Trust me, it's a fun ride ... for me at least.

I grip the cold handle of the casket. The crisp white gloves we were given help protect my hands from the Seattle winter. My five cousins and I lift all at once. It is much heavier than I expected, but for a man of a hundred and forty pounds, I

Dark Whisper: The Fire That Burns Within

Thoughts of my bare hands on her body tempt me, but I am always in control. Her back arches from the feel of the cold leather touching her skin. Her eyes open and she looks at me with familiar eyes. She sits up and tries to lean into me. With my hand on her chest, I gently push her back to her pillow. Slowly, I run my hands up her arms, pushing them above her head. The smile on her face shows she knows what is coming next. I reach under her pillow and pull out three silk scarves. Crossing her wrists, I bind her to the headboard. Ever so slowly, I run my hand down her golden tan body, trying my best not to become aroused.

As my hand passes over her freshly shaved pussy, I feel the heat through my gloves. She is where I want her to be. I make my way back to the foot of the bed. There is little to no work spreading her legs to the far corners of the mattress. With the two remaining scarves, I secure her ankles to the frame. In the moon's light, I see the glistening moisture dripping off her swollen lips. Inserting the middle finger on my left hand into her, there is no resistance. Her moans make it impossible for me not to want to kill her. I put my right hand firmly over her mouth and nose and squeeze. There's the look I'm here to see—

hold my own. Around me I see crying. Even the other pallbearers have tears in their eyes.

It's time to put on my best sad face and continue to walk in pace with the others. I can't help but wonder how many pallbearers I've given work to and how many graves have been dug because of my handy work. With those thoughts, I can't help but to smile. I quickly suppress the joy that comes over me because this is not the time or place for these kinds of thoughts.

We walk slowly and reverently past friends and family, and I can't help but feel like my ability to show emotions are on trial. The lack of time I spent with him, and the fact that I did not know him well, will play in my favor when the question of no tears come up. The walk to this hole in the ground seems forever away, and then there's the question of what we do when we get there.

It's not a normal Seattle day. The sun is shining, and there are almost no clouds in the sky. Such a nice day. Too bad I'm stuck here playing human. I look at this thing that everyone is doing, this crying thing. Does it really help them feel better or is it just another attempt at showing that they care? I guess saying it is not enough.

RUFUS MONTGOMERY JR.

Then there's the "I'm sorry" that they tell us family. I didn't know him well, so why say sorry to me? And why are you sorry? Did you do it? Come to think of it, how many times should I have said sorry because I did do it? There was that one time I went to the funeral. Who would have guessed I gave them the guest of honor? And if I remember correctly, I said sorry for their loss, but I left out how I carefully planned his death. How much fun would it have been if I told them?

As for this grief, what's it all about? Do people really miss the dead as much as they would like others to think, or am I doing them a favor? Stay with me here. We've all thought to ourselves, "Man, I wish he or she were dead." Now let's just say someone like me comes along and makes that happen for you. You're welcome. Do you show up at their place of rest and talk about how great of a person they were, or the piece of crap they truly were? Or better yet, bake me a cake and send a thank you note. Then, they would have to know who I am and what I've done, and we can't have that.

As I look around, it seems like everyone is competing to have cared for this person the most. You always hear how good and special a person is when they're dead, but we all know they were average at best. As for being a good person, that has always been in question. All the time I hear people ask, "Why do bad things happen to good people?" Who are these "good people" everyone is talking about? From first glance, others would say how nice of a guy I seem. After a while, they will say I am a pleasure to be around. With all that said, I'm as bad as they come. Only when you're looking up at me feeling your heart beating out of control will you think, "Maybe he's not that nice a guy." That is the point when good people are not good anymore, and that's when it's too late.

God, when are we going to put this coffin down! Are we walking this slowly so everyone can get a good look? I've heard all day how great of a man he was when he was alive, but I did my research. The underage girls he partook in may not say the same about him, nor would his wife, and don't make me get into the gambling he did. Now that she's got a look at her now gambling debts, his wife is probably crying because she didn't get the chance to kill him herself.

It's not like I have trust issues or anything like that. I just don't trust anyone. The way I see it, these good people that I

RUFUS MONTGOMERY JR.

hear about are just bad people that haven't done bad yet. That's probably why it's so easy to do what I do.

Finally!

"Do we just put it on the straps?" Good, put him over the grave. I thought I would never be rid of that thing. Worst part is these people think they and I have something in common—that being the loss they feel. Only thing I've lost this trip is sleep.

I sit with my cousins because it looks like the right thing to do. My dad is sitting with his siblings, and all my cousins are sitting together, comforting one another. People say I look like my father. We share the almond-shaped eyes, although he is darker than me. I have my mother's shade of brown. People always ask me what happened to my hair. I could tell them I cut it to keep from leaving evidence, but instead, I tell them I look good bald. At around five-foot-eight, I am not the runt of the litter, but I don't tower over anyone either.

Being the oldest boy of a Caribbean family comes with responsibilities. Like, making sure I made it to this funeral no matter what plans I had. Oh well, I have some fun planned for later.

Dark Whisper: The Fire That Burns Within

Now they want to comfort me. I guess I'll let them do what it is they do Now, there's hand holding. I hope this is over soon. I need to kill something and soon before I lose my mind. Some would say I've already lost my mind. Especially if they had any idea of the things I have done. If they only knew this hand they're holding has taken bodies apart and has snapped the necks of unsuspecting victims. I savor the thought of a warm neck in my hands, the blood pumping through their veins, and the knowledge that I can and will bring that to an end. I think I will make that one of the first things I do when I get back. But why should I wait? There's someone here that needs to be shown death. I'm sure I can find someone I like.

Who to pick? How will I do it? I will start by looking for someone who will go the most unnoticed. I'll befriend them, then bring them in and make them the life of the party, or in this case, a funeral. Let me see...

Okay, there. Her over there crying alone. Is she family or a friend of the family? Don't want to kill off family members now do I? Yet, if that option were on the table, this would be so much easier because I'm looking at a few I would love to end right now. Back to the plan. After making them the life of the

RUFUS MONTGOMERY JR.

party, I can go unnoticed and sneak away. Then I can find my real victim. The others should be busy with the newcomer. Can't go too far because I'm on foot. There are some shopping centers close to here. I could always find that lonely shopper and kill them in their car. Then there's the possibility of finding a walker who comes this way every day and has his guard down. That alone will make him easy prey. People get very comfortable in their everyday routine and that makes my job that much easier. Comfort means your guard is down and you won't see me coming, and when you do, it's too late. There they go again. God, does someone else really have more words to say about this guy? Oh yeah, it's for sure—someone needs to die.

Dark Whisper: The Fire That Burns Within

2

WHEN PEOPLE ARE FACED WITH DEATH, they usually start off with a look of disbelief. The blood leaves their face, their jaw relaxes, and tears fill their eyes. They can't believe what is happening. This is where they separate themselves from each other. We will start with the pleading man, whom I really hate. He tells you about his kids that I know he beats, and one of them isn't even his. But he doesn't know I know. He pleads for his wife and what is she going to do without him. I'm thinking the same thing she's been doing the entire time for the last six years—her three-year-old's father.

Then there are the ones that go straight to offering me money. If they only knew how much I have access to. I'm in it for the blood. When they're done bribing me, they assume someone put me up to it. Then, we're back to money ... and he's going to double what I'm being paid. Oh man, it's fun! I think

RUFUS MONTGOMERY JR.

what kind of person this is. Why does he think someone wants him dead? Now, it really gets good. I know how much he has and can give me, so I say I'm getting paid well over what he has and see where he goes from there. Let's just say he offers me money he doesn't have, which is fine with me because I'm not here for the money and he dies thinking someone he knows had him killed. I'm an equal opportunity kind of guy.

There are the women that offer things the men don't or won't. Well, there was that one guy who thought outside the box to save his own ass. Some of that stuff I'm pretty sure a man can't do, but I killed him just to stop him from trying to explain.

As for women, there is the crying and pleading. They tell me their name over and over, trying to make me see them as a human and not a plaything. If I did not see them as human, I would not have taken the time to kill them. After calming her down, she starts telling me about her step kids but leaves out the part that she herself didn't want kids. If it weren't for the kid's father's bank account being as big as it was, she wouldn't have let him touch her, much less put up with his kids. The kids and the husband can thank me later because she was going to clean him out in the divorce he didn't know was coming.

Dark Whisper: The Fire That Burns Within

As for church people, they are very boring. They call for God. I wait, they wait, God doesn't show. I kill them and that's that. Home in time for bed.

Down in the ground he goes. Maybe we get to eat soon. Oh no! It looks like there's going to be hugging. Why hugging?

Who is this lady coming this way? She's putting her arms around me. It better be quick, cause if this woman does not stop hugging me in the next two seconds, I will have found my next victim. The touching and hugging is too much for me. I can manage some human contact, but I like to be the one in control of that. Let me explain the problem. Some may see hugging as a show of affection, but I see it as torture. Those seconds of having another human holding me feels like a lifetime. Not knowing when or even if they are going to let go brings about physical pain unlike anything I can put into words.

You're probably thinking I wasn't hugged enough as a child. If you think that, you would be very wrong. I was hugged a lot, and I loved it. The same people who hugged me as a child can do it now and I would love it just the same. But, leaving that up to someone else, I find myself wanting to kill someone.

RUFUS MONTGOMERY JR.

"Thank you, I really needed that," I tell her as I wipe the fake tears from my eyes and hurry away. They think I'm too upset to be bothered. Perfect. With my side hobby, I've learned how to pretend. I find it very useful to be able to read people's moods and personalities. Mood tells me how open they are. The more open, the easier the prey. As for their personality, do I want to take the time to kill them? That is what I find most interesting—the part where no one sees me for what I am until it's too late. Far too often we hear, "I never thought he would do such a thing!" They say this as the police find bodies buried in shallow graves in a killer's backyard. Or, when they realize that meat they couldn't quite put a taste to was the girl that went missing three months prior. Surprise! She made it to the BBQ after all. At least she didn't die for nothing. A little BBQ sauce and she found her calling.

All this talk about food is making me hungry. Hold on! I hope you don't think I eat people, because I don't like food or the disgusting process of eating very much. I simply eat to live, not live to eat. As I was saying, most of us go unnoticed to the untrained eye, and to most of the best trained eyes as well, but you won't find them admitting to that. It's always fun watching them miss the obvious.

They say that people like me do what we do because we can't help ourselves or that we really don't know or understand why we have that deep need to kill. Well, there is one other reason no one wants to or likes to admit. It's a scary reason to face. I don't have a deep need to kill. I want to kill. I kill when I'm bored. It's fun for me. Then there is what happens when it's all over and there I am alone with a dead body. After all the screams, and the "please don't kill me," I'm done, and the fun has ended. I don't stand there thinking, "Why did I do this? Why do I end lives?" It's not a question I need to ask because I have the best reason of them all, and that's the one that scares us the most. I don't lie to myself and say I couldn't help myself. No, I am fully aware what I'm doing is wrong. I know what it does and how it affects others and their lives. So, you ask why I do it? One simple answer; I like it. I love the work that I do. Don't feel left out because it could be you. The other question is how I select my prey. That's another fun story that may have you checking the back seat of your car before getting in. That's fine with me. I like for you to see me coming.

RUFUS MONTGOMERY JR.

Let's face it, how fun would it be if I didn't get to see the look on your face? I'm sure you're asking yourself who are the lucky ones? Or shall I say the unlucky ones? Some have a type and only partake of that one flavor—that's the need thing I was talking about. It's a lack of control of who or when or if they kill. It almost takes away the chorus. I'm not a control freak—I do not fool myself into thinking I can control most of what happens around me. As for my emotions, they are mine and mine alone to control. What I mean is any outside stimuli—like developing feelings for someone or even anger brought about from the actions of another person affecting me—would be the same as giving control of me and who I am to someone or something else. Like the man whose head I put a bag over and sealed it by duct taping his neck. I sat in front of him and watched until the bag no longer inflated.

Then there's the woman I strangled with her seatbelt as I watched her face in the rear-view mirror. Why her? Why him? I don't see why not. I saw him in a bookstore. He was a fairly nice guy, but when he was leaving, he saw no reason to hold the door for a lady with a stroller. When the door shut on her, it knocked the baby's cup out of the cup holder. That deserved my attention. What kind of man does that? I followed him out of the store, and the rest you already know.

As for the woman, they tell you texting and driving is dangerous, but they never tell you it's because you will miss the man climbing into your back seat at the stoplight. With eyes fixed on the phone, she didn't see the "door open" light on the dash. The music was so loud she didn't hear me close the door behind me. With this, timing is everything. When it was all done, I texted that friend saying, "She won't be meeting you later."

He replied, "Why not? Who is this?"

I answered, "She's dead. We all hear how texting and driving is dangerous. She just found out how dangerous." Then I added, "You're not driving right now, are you?" Needless to say, I got no reply.

Oh, great. My dad is calling me over to meet someone. I do hope there's not going to be more hugging. I wonder sometimes if he sees the real me, and in our case is it true what they say, "Like father like son?"

"I'll be right there, dad." I hurry over to him. Yes, I do kill people, but I do still try to be a good son.

RUFUS MONTGOMERY JR.

I take my place at his side. Unlike me, my dad is a big guy. He stands about six feet, and easily puts his hands over my shoulder. At that point, I go from a man of twenty-five to a boy of fifteen. I think that may be what keeps him from seeing the face of my dark whisper.

"Are you doing ok, dad?" I ask. He's just lost a brother. He tightens his hand on my shoulder.

"I'm fine, son," he replies, slightly pushing me forward to introduce me to a woman standing in front of us. Someone said she was a friend of the family or something like that. My grandmother is looking over here. She knows something about this woman that we do not. With a quick once over, I can tell a few things about her myself. She's not as sad as she would like us to think. She has a napkin that hasn't been used, and her makeup is not disturbed one bit. As many times as I've seen her wipe her nose, there should be a bit of rawness, but there is none.

The skill of noticing what most people miss comes in handy for my side occupation. I'm like a Sherlock Holmes and Jack the Ripper all in one. I see one more thing that I'm sure my dad picked up on. The way her right shoulder is angled at him, he may get lucky. Noticing her interest in my dad doesn't help with my normal level of emotional discomfort that saturates the air around me.

"Very nice to meet you." I extend my hand.

"How old are you now?" she asks as she proceeds past my outstretched hand to come in for a hug. "You were a boy the last time I saw you," she adds.

Now, I'm a man that kills. Would you like to see? I stop breathing as every muscle in my body tightens. Over this woman's shoulder, my grandmother recognizes the look on my face. She makes her way over.

"I think I could really go for one of those hugs. Can I have my grandson, please?" She reaches out her hands for me.

Free at last! I'm safe with grandma. I can breathe again.

"Come, boys. It's time to eat." Granny looks at the woman, and to my surprise says, "That's some good makeup you have there. It held up through all the crying you were doing."

Here I am, a killer saved by his granny. How embarrassing.

We walk away, leaving my dad and that woman to talk for a moment longer. I look at my grandmother and recognize that face. As we get further away, I glance back to see my father and the woman following us.

"I know you didn't know him very well, so I don't expect you to be bothered by all of this. I don't know about everyone else, but I'm so happy you're here for your father," my grandmother says.

"Here is where I needed to be, grandmother. My family needs me," I reply.

It's strange. She is the only person who hasn't tried to comfort me for a loss I wasn't feeling. As we walk to the dining hall, we pass friends and family that stop us to talk and comfort my grandmother for the loss of her son. I look on as they occasionally address me and tell me sorry. Each time, my grandmother squeezes my hand as I'm bombarded with all these emotions. Emotions themselves don't bother me—it's the lack most people have of controlling them that makes my face the last thing some people see.

I am really going to find out who here is not family. I must make sure their untimely death won't put me at another one of these things. My grandmother seems detached. Can she really be like me? Can she kill people? In her younger days, could she have held the throat of another person and watched the life leave their eyes? Why do I find that so hard to believe? I've done it many times. My grandmother can't be killer—she babysat me. I wonder how close I was to a pillow over my face on the nights I wouldn't stop crying.

"What's so funny?" my grandmother asks.

I didn't realize I was laughing out loud. "Nothing. I was just thinking about something funny."

Why does the thought of my demise as a child by my grandmother's hand and a well-placed pillow make me laugh? I am a serial killer, after all. That could be why.

"I know you don't have a genuine reason to be as sad as the people that did know him," she says out of nowhere. "But I thank you for playing the part as well as you have been. Everyone is buying it. Keep up the good work."

She can tell, but how? Hell, my dad has no idea. He keeps telling me, "It's going to be okay, son."

I want to say, "I know, he didn't do much when he was alive!" But then I remember I'm playing human. I stop and think. Those people that saw the inhumane side of me weren't going to live much longer after seeing my face. When they see that face, they stop seeing me as a who and start seeing me as a what. Can you look at someone and see that they are capable of evil just from the look on their face? Most people can't, but I now ask myself, "Can my grandmother hear my dark whisper? Does she listen to her own whisper the same way I do mine?"

Right now, it's not my dark whisper that's talking to me—it's my stomach. It seems like everyone is going to stop us before we get to eat. I notice my grandmother hasn't had much to say to my uncle's wife. Now, I have to wonder if my grandmother knew about the gambling and the other women, and if so, who else knew? I think I've found something to do. I don't care too much that he died, but the how is worth looking into. While doing that, maybe I'll find someone that I like. Even so, that woman that seems to want nothing more than to comfort my dad will be my fallback kill. I hope he doesn't get too attached to her.

"How does she know dad and uncle?" I ask my grandmother, hoping she knows something that can help.

"I'm not really sure. I think they worked together, but there is something about her..." Grandma gives her another glance. Does she see what I see and are we thinking the same thing? Do we both want to kill this woman just because? I hope my dad brings her to our table. That way, I can learn more about my prey. I can go sit with my cousins, but that won't be much fun, plus I really have nothing in common with them. What would we talk about? College and what major we're picking this semester? Or we can talk about the people we're seeing, or how great they are. Then there's the talk about jobs and what we are all doing. These are all things I do not wish to share with them—things some of which may have me reconsidering my rule of not killing family.

Wanting nothing more than the chance to show up the person sitting next to me isn't a game I want to be a part of. Finding a life to take, now that may make this trip worth it. Here I am smiling again. My cousins know I'm different, but they don't know in what way. Their need to be the favorite and most liked in the family is quite quaint, but pathetic. It gets fun to watch, though. Here comes my dad and the dead lady.

"Grandma, I'm going to sit with my dad and that woman."

"What are you up to, young man? Don't you want to sit with your cousins?" she asks me.

RUFUS MONTGOMERY JR.

"Now, what would be the fun in that?" I ask my grandmother.

She looks at me again with that look on her face, like she can see me, like she knows that woman is as good as dead. "Have fun."

As I walk away to sit with my dad, I hear, "Let me know if you find out anything good."

I look back to see that look again on her face. "Oh, I will let you know what I find out." I do hope I at least get to kill her by myself. I'm not sure I'm ready to team up with my grandmother yet. Lucky for me, there's a free seat next to her. I walk over and sit right across from her. This way, not only will I be able to gage her voice, I'll also be able to read her face. Shall I start my game where she ends up dead? I lean forward, and with a smile on my face, I get to the point.

"How did you know my uncle?"

3

SHE LOOKS AT ME AS IF I JUST ASKED HER AGE. She isn't sure how to answer. Maybe it's because my dad is sitting next to her, and she doesn't want him to know. I really thought it would take her longer to bleed, but there is blood in the water, and I can smell it.

"You two must have been close. I see how hard you're taking it. You and my aunt must be close as well," I add. Why stop with bleeding if I can make her hemorrhage? My dad looks at her and leans forward, equally interested in hearing her answer. But, soon my dad, being that nice guy that he is, tries to tourniquet the bleeding by changing subjects. This niceness of his is something I did not inherit.

"Do you have any kids?" he asks.

Here I am trying to hunt, and here he is trying to help my prey get away. Hope he's not hunting for her as well. That will make for an interesting chase. Yet, I don't think we are thinking about the same end for her. I can't blame him or my uncle—she is a good-looking woman. Maybe if I weren't looking for something to do, or in this case undo, my dad would be interested in the same end result for this one. No matter, this time we have different plans, and nothing he does is going to stop the bleeding.

"I have two kids," she answers. She's relieved my questions have stopped, but little does she know they are far from over! I notice a missing wedding ring, but still see that it wasn't long ago it was removed. I see the groove a ring leaves when someone puts on a little weight.

"Was your husband not able to come with you to the funeral?" And now we have more blood. I love the smell of fear.

As I watch her breathing change and the color leave her cheeks, I know I'm right back where I need to be. Now I even have my dad interested in her answer. God, I wish grandma were here to see her boy work.

"We are no longer together," she says, rubbing her ring finger. "This is his weekend with the kids," she adds.

Dark Whisper: The Fire That Burns Within

Time to draw her in by pulling back and showing her my softer side that doesn't really exist. I will now be kind.

"That's terrible to hear. First a husband and now a friend? No wonder you're this upset. Well, I'm sorry for your losses. I hope things start looking up for you soon." As I speak, I can see her relax. I now have the information I need to know if she is lying or not. Now we really play. My mind wonders. I look down at her perfectly brown flesh. It's intoxicating. Everything seems to move in slow motion. The feeling is unreal.

I reach for my sharpest knife. Slowly, I moisten my lips with my tongue, wanting nothing more than to run my hands across that warm flesh. I control myself, and instead, I rub the icy blade ever so gently over the sweating meat, looking for that sweet spot. Even you would know it when you find it. You don't need to be a killer to recognize where to make that first cut. There it is! I raise my elbow and arch my wrist. At first, I push down, and with every pull, I become a little more aggressive. Right on time the fuel of life shows itself—so red and so thick. My steak is rare. Just like I like it.

"Is your food ok, son?" my father asks.

Did he see the joy I took in cutting this steak?

RUFUS MONTGOMERY JR.

"It's great, dad. Just like I like it." I try to look normal. "Just a little red in this one spot, that's all." This can soon be her. Look at her. Is her food good as well? All last meals should be enjoyable. I find it hard to hide how annoyed I am that she is still breathing. Every breath she takes taunts me. I'm sure if I take the time to look around this room, I'll find many worthy of death.

Noticing how everyone is being fake when they think no one is looking, they stop playing this game of who can cry the hardest and who misses him the most. Now that the suffering is over, there are sounds of laughter. I close my eyes and imagine each one of their laughs as screams. It's like a lullaby to me. How quickly our sorrows are forgotten. Laughter replaces the sound of crying. She, who seemed inconsolable, now sits across from me, openly flirting with my dad. I now believe that my dead uncle was her lover.

Here she is, gently caressing the back of my father's hand. She looks at him with a smile across her face, when just moments ago she grieved my uncle. This one will die badly–I will see to it. Some would think me inhumane if they only knew the things I have done. I do what most in this room only dream of doing. I am as I am, and I embrace who I am. They pretend for their own selfish reasons. They think no one would like them if they only knew the real them. With all that said, I like myself just fine.

As annoying as her fakeness is, I still find her appealing. Her soft almond colored skin, her full lips ... if my uncle wasn't sleeping with her, I'm sure it wasn't because of the lack of trying. Her body is not a body of a fifty-year-old, and I'm only guessing her age based on her knowing my dad from the past. From what I saw earlier, her ass aged very well, and if I'm not being fooled by a well-made bra, her breasts are perfect. I've decided I want to see them. If she's to be the one, I really can't let my dad get attached. Hopefully, breaking her down the way I did made him lose interest. Now to see if I can change what she must think of me after that little game.

"Your kids must be young. How old are they?"

"No, they're not that young. They are thirteen and sixteen," she says nervously.

"Wow!" I lean in close. "You don't look old enough to have kids that old." Not giving her a chance to recover from the compliment, I ask, "Girls, boys?"

RUFUS MONTGOMERY JR.

"What?" she asks.

"The kids. Are they girls or boys?"

"The 16-year-old is a boy, and the 13-year-old is a girl."

"You're in trouble if she's as beautiful as her mother." And just like that, I have her. She leans in to hear everything I have to say next, and it only gets better. We go on talking and I fake laugh a few times. I've learned very well over the years how to be exactly what people need me to be. Here I am again, playing human. Her laugh is not as annoying as I found it just moments ago. Now, it's entertaining.

"Dad, when are you leaving back to England? I know you're not looking forward to that flight," I say, pointing out the distance between her and my dad.

"I'll be here for three more days. You are right about the flight. It is long and I am not looking forward to it."

"How long are you going to be in Washington?" She's asking me what I want to hear. Just when I think my dad will be mad, I see pride in his face. He's proud of his boy. Sitting here, I can feel several eyes on me, but one set of eyes stands out from the rest. I know my family doesn't know exactly how to take me, but I don't give a shit. As long as they stay out of my way, there will be no problem. From the corner of my eye, I see my grandmother smiling at me. I think she may have been watching me.

"Excuse me, I'm going to check on my grandmother." As I walk away, I can hear them talking.

"He really loves his grandmother, doesn't he?"

"Yes, he does. She seems to understand him better than the rest of us. I think they're a lot alike in ways we don't quite understand."

I can't help but to smile when I hear him say that. You have no idea, dad.

My grandmother shakes her head and asks, "What are you saying to that woman that has her unable to take her eyes off of you?"

"Really?" I ask.

Grandma grabs my arm. "Don't look back, not yet."

Pretending not to notice, grandmother watches for the perfect moment for me to turn and give the woman the attention she so wants. I can't help but to wonder once again how my grandmother is so versed in this game I'm playing.

RUFUS MONTGOMERY JR.

"Ok, look now, she is about to pop," grandmother says jokingly.

When I look over, eye contact is instant. It's almost like she's fixed on me, worried she will miss me stealing a look at her.

"Don't look too long, boy. Leave her wanting."

"How do you even know what I'm doing over there?" I hope for an answer that would show me her skills at vetting a victim. Is my grandmother a killer, or have I just been seeing what I want to see? It would be nice to have just one person who gets me.

"I have eyes, boy, and I was young once. I see you're looking for something to do. I get it. You're young and curious, and she is a good-looking woman. You seem to have her right where you want her." She winks at me.

I'm a serial killer, but this is not a conversation I wish to have with my granny.

"Grandma, please, we are not having this talk." I let out a genuine laugh. Even with being dead inside, a laugh feels good when I can have one.

"I notice you drove here by yourself. Did you not stay with your father at your aunt's house?" Once again, my grandmother shows she doesn't miss a thing.

"No, I got a room at a hotel not too far from here, and it's still pretty close to the airport. I prefer to have my own space. That way, I have somewhere to retreat to when I've had my fill of human contact."

By her nods, I can tell she understands what I mean.

"I heard your cousins talking about going out later, after all of this. Do you plan on joining them tonight?"

"No. I have a thing," I reply.

Looking around at the table, my grandmother asks, "Is she this thing you have?"

"Grandma, I said we're not having that talk, and no, she's not the thing. It's something I've been meaning to do for a while now."

"I hope this thing proves to be just as much fun as that other thing at that table."

"Not letting up are you, granny? I think it's time to leave. This thing I have is going to take time, and I don't want to be late."

RUFUS MONTGOMERY JR.

"Ok, boy, just don't leave before saying goodbye." She motions for me to kiss her on the cheek.

"Of course, I can't leave without saying bye to my number one girl." I kiss my grandmother and return to my table to put the finishing touches on this game I'm playing. "Dad, I must be leaving."

"So soon?" he asks. "I thought we would have more time to talk."

Here she sits, looking up at me like an innocent deer caught in headlights. From her reaction to the news of my leaving, I can tell she doesn't want this to be the last time she sees me. This same woman that's been faking all day, I've managed to pull real feelings from her. I think to myself how fun this is going to be.

"Son, you're not going out with the others later?" my dad asks.

"No, I'm going back to my room to rest. Maybe get some work done later. I still have a lot going on back home and I don't want to fall behind."

"You're not staying with family?" she asks, sounding almost excited.

"I'm staying at a hotel close by. I think it's the Lance Lake Hotel, the big one."

"The one by that gourmet coffee shop?" she asks.

"Yes, that one. Room 427." Do you like how I did that? I answered her question without her even having to ask. I even saw a smile creep across her face.

"I must be leaving. I have some stops to make before getting back to my room." As I make my way to the door, I can see my cousins looking at me. I could go over and tell them bye, but to hell with them. They'll just have to do with a wave and a smile. As I clear the threshold, I can feel the full me, the killer, rushing back into me. It's like a shot of adrenalin bringing me back to life. I even feel my walk change back to my normal strut. I no longer have to play human—I can be the animal that I truly am—the kind of animal that holds life and death in his hands. I climb into the rental and make sure the GPS is turned off and disconnected. Even though they don't have my real name, I still do not want a record of where this car and I travel.

On my way back to the hotel, I pay a homeless man a hundred dollars to buy me a burner phone.

RUFUS MONTGOMERY JR.

"Thank you, and here's that money I promised you. Keep the change."

I drive far out of my way to make a well-needed phone call. You remember I said I had that thing? It's been about an hour since I left the funeral, and I'm just getting back to the hotel to get ready to start my night. I do my best work in the dark. I walk through the lobby, trying to draw as little attention as possible. I notice this gorgeous woman at the bar. She catches me looking and smiles. I smile back and think to myself, another time.

I make it up to my room and put down my go bag. My go bag is just a bag I always have with me. At first glance, it looks empty, but in it is everything I need to kill and cover. I go to the bathroom to pee and to start taking off some of my costume. As I'm washing my hands, I hear a knock at the door. I'm not expecting anyone, at least not this early. I look through the peephole and am pleasantly surprised to see it worked all too well. I think about putting my shirt back on but decide not to.

I open the door and invite her in. I guess someone could say something, but what's the point? I don't want to talk to her, and I don't think she is here for that either. I close the door behind me and wonder, if she knew what I have planned for her earlier today, would she have made it this easy for me?"

She rubs her hand down my naked chest and looks me in the eyes. I place my hand on the small of her back and pull her close. I slowly lean in and kiss her nose. Gently, I reach down and let my hand make the climb up her tightly fitted dress. I make my way around and up her inner thighs. When I get to the front laces of her damp panties, I can already feel how wet she is.

"You did that to me at the table," she says as she spreads her legs, making it easier for me to get to her.

I rub her panties, getting some of her juices on my fingers. With my left hand behind her head, I take the wet fingers on my other hand and rub it on her beautiful, puckered lips. Before she knows what is happening, I'm sucking the wet off of them. I reach down and pull that black dress up over her head, then walk her over to the bed. I lay her down with her legs still hanging off the edge. I caress her calves and slowly remove her shoes, revealing her equally sexy, well-painted toes. I unhook her bra and free her breasts. They are all I hoped they would be. I can't keep my tongue off the perfect nipples. With her hands firmly on the back of my head, I can hear her heavy breathing. I now know it is time for her to be liberated from the confinement of her underwear. She arches her back, making it easy for me to remove them. After pulling them around her feet, she quickly leans up and starts working on my belt. Before I know it, my pants are at my feet and she's vigorously taking me in her mouth, making it extremely difficult to step out of them. As I caress her face, I feel her hand on my backside, pulling me harder into her mouth. It's my turn to be violent. Gently pulling her warm, wet mouth off me, I push her back down on the bed. She puts her feet on my chest and pushes herself up to the top of it, before turning over. Gripping the headboard, she pulls herself up onto her knees and looks back at me.

"I hope you didn't have too much to eat earlier," she says, as she spreads her legs apart.

"Not at all," I reply. "I always save room for a taste of that. From where I'm standing, that looks tasty." I climb on to the bed, making my way up to her glistening pussy. Moving in closer to the welcoming promise of pleasure, I smell sweet lavender. Her back arches when she feels my tongue press against her inner thigh. She spreads her legs wider, giving me more room to work my tongue up and down her slit. The sound of her hands tightening around the bedpost fills the room. As I gently tap her clit with kisses, she lets out a moan as her legs shake. Grabbing her legs firmly, I drive my tongue further inside. With the sound of licking, sucking, and kissing echoing throughout the room, I can feel her body going limp. I lose myself for a moment in the taste of her. As she comes close to climax, I get up and slowly enter her in time to feel her pulsating around me. Pressing my lips on her cheeks, I whisper, "I'm not finished with you yet."

With one hand holding her in position, and the other helping her keep hold of the bedpost, I thrust slowly and firmly into her until we are both spent and collapse to the bed. As I lay next to her hearing her breath, I think how easy it would be to end her here and now, but it's late, and I should get going. She is asleep, but this still works. She will make for a great alibi. I quietly get up and dress myself as not to wake her. I need her still asleep and here when I get back. I grab my go bag and think to myself, I wonder if she makes cookies?

I told you I had a thing.

RUFUS MONTGOMERY JR.

USING A FOLDED NEWSPAPER, HE BRUSHED the bits off the dashboard and vowed to clean it up later. But by the pile that was still left on the floor, it was evident he'd been saying that for a long time. As he pulled up to the two-story house, the onslaught of blue and red lights danced on his face. With the lack of detail that was given to him over the phone about the situation, he could tell that there was a dead body in the house.

"This way." The officer waved him over to an open spot between two police cars.

"Are you ever going to light that thing?" The officer asked as he opened the door of the white poorly painted convertible.

"I can't stand the smell of these things burning," he said, placing a chewed-up cigar in his cup holder.

Dark Whisper: The Fire That Burns Within

"What's going on in there? I wasn't given much detail over the phone on this one. You're going to have to get me up to speed."

"Yes sir," the young officer replied, shutting the car door.

"I told you to call me Stone." He dusted a cigar bit off his khaki pants.

"Yes, I forgot sir ... I mean, Detective Stone."

"Just Stone." He laughed. "Take me to the body."

As they walked to the house, they had to dodge the forensic team going in and out the front door. Stone noticed one of the officers questioning a very distraught man over by the mailbox with his hands in the air and pacing back and forth.

"Keith, who is that?" Stone pointed over to where the noise was coming from. "And why is he so upset?" He stopped to see if he could make out what the man was saying.

"Oh him, he found the body."

"And who is he to the dead person in the house?" Stone asked.

Keith pulled a small notepad out of his left uniform pocket. "It says here that he's the husband."

"And why wasn't he home?"

RUFUS MONTGOMERY JR.

Keith looked closer at his notes as Stone pulled out a small black flashlight and shined it onto Keith's notebook. "Thank you. It looks like they're separated, and he doesn't live here at the moment. He came over when he couldn't get her on her cell phone the last two days. He said he thought she just didn't want to talk to him."

"So, I take it that it's not a friendly breakup?" A loud click went off along with the light. "Don't let him leave till we get a chance to speak to him." As Stone turned to enter the house, he almost bumped into one of the forensics working the scene. "Oh, sorry, buddy."

"No problem, sir," a woman's voice came from behind the mask.

Stone cleared his throat. "You're a woman."

She removed the surgical mask and pulled back the hood that revealed long red hair. "I was last time I checked. It's ok, in this getup, who could know what's under here? If you're going in there, you're going to want to put these on." She handed them paper boots to put over their shoes along with two pairs of blue latex gloves. "Try not to mess up my scene." She smiled and walked over to the van where they were keeping evidence.

Stone looked at Keith. Keith shrugged his shoulders and smiled. "I was going to give you some booties and gloves."

Stone shook the gloves at Keith. "You making me look bad, kid."

As they entered the house, the faint smell of potpourri lingered in the air. The plush of the carpet shifted under foot with every step. The paper shoe covers made it almost feel like they were walking on water. As they walked over to the stairs, Stone noticed the scissors on the coffee table. What he found strange was that the closer they got to the staircase, the colder it became.

Keith stopped and pointed. "The last room on the right."

Everyone Stone passed had the same look on their face—the look of confusion. As he entered the room, the sweet smell of strawberries filled his nose. This is not the kind of murder scene he was used to. As he moved closer to the bed, he could not quite make out what he was looking at. The flash from the forensics' camera made him have to squint to see the body between flashes.

RUFUS MONTGOMERY JR.

"Oh, sorry, Stone. I didn't hear you come in. This damn carpet makes it hard to hear anything, much less to move around in these paper shoes."

"That's okay, Larry. Get the pictures you need." Stone walked around the room. Nothing out of place and no sign of a struggle or a fight of any kind. I'm sure she did not tie herself up. She's naked and it seems she wanted to be that way. "Larry, have you guys removed anything from the room, maybe ripped clothing?"

"No, the room is just like we found it."

The sound of the gloves snapping down on his wrist caused Larry to look over at Stone who was looking down at the bed. He pulled up the collar on the back of his jacket. The cold Seattle air blew on his neck through the open window.

"Did someone sit on the bed? Here it looks like someone heavier than her sat on this part of the bed. Get a picture of this for me. Were there any prints in here that aren't hers?" Stone examined the window.

The forensic investigator focused the lens to take a photo. He leaned over to get a better shot. A barrage of flashes went off. "That's the strange thing. There aren't any fingerprints."

"You guys only found her prints?" Stone asked.

"No, that's not what I'm saying. There are no fingerprints of any kind in here. It's like no one opened the door or the window. Do you smell the strawberry scent that fills the room? Well, it's lotion. We dusted the bottle and found nothing. If we weren't looking at her lying there, there would be no proof that she was ever in this room."

"How is that even possible? When you get her back to the morgue, make sure they run a whole rape kit on her. There has to be something of him left here." As he walked to the door, trying not to succumb to the slippery paper shoes on the carpet. "Keith!" His voice sounded down the stairs. There he saw Keith talking to the redhead he almost bumped into not twenty minutes ago.

"Look at this guy." Stone laughed and shook his head. "Excuse me sir can I have my officer back?"

"He's all yours," she replied as she tucked her long red hair back into the hood.

"Now, now, you two. No need to fight over me," Keith said, handing back her mask as she fixed her hood.

"I just don't like when my date wonders off," Stone said as he walked past them to the kitchen. "Do I smell oatmeal cookies?"

"Yes, and if you look, six of them are missing," the redhead said.

"So, she likes cookies," Keith said.

"We thought that too until we spoke to the husband. Yes, she likes to bake cookies, but she wouldn't eat these."

"Why is that?' Stone asked.

She walked over to the tray of cookies. Pulling the flashlight off of Keith's belt and shining it on one of them. "If you look closely, you will see there are raisins in these cookies."

Leaning over to get a better look, Stone raised his shoulders and looked to her with anticipation.

"After talking to her husband, he told us she despised raisins, so she would not have eaten one of them, much less six."

"Let me see that flashlight?" Stone pointed out a gel-like substance. "Get a swab of that, I want to know what that is." He handed Keith his light and headed to the door.

"Where are you going?" Keith asked.

"To talk to the husband. Something is missing, and it's not just six cookies."

Stone trotted down the steep driveway. The steps leading from the front door were not fast enough for him—he was a man with questions that needed answers. As he got closer, he could hear the husband ask the officer, "Who is he?"

Stone shook the man's hand. "I am Detective Stone, the lead on this case. I am so sorry for your loss, and I plan on finding out who did this to you and your family." Stone released his grip, reached inside his pocket, and pulled out a notepad and a shiny pen that looked like it has a lot of miles on it. "I have a few questions I need answered to better help me understand what happened in there. First of all, what is your favorite kind of cookie?"

"Are you kidding me? What the hell does that have to do with my dead wife? How is that going to help anything?" He turned to walk away.

"Oatmeal cookies!"

The man stopped. "Oatmeal?"

RUFUS MONTGOMERY JR.

"Yes, oatmeal raisin, two trays of them." Stone walked over to him.

"Peanut butter," the man whispered.

"Excuse me? What was that?" Stone asked as he jotted it down.

"Peanut butter cookies are my favorite. She hated raisins. As long as I've known her, she's never baked oatmeal anything."

"Not even for the kids?"

He lowered his head. "We didn't have any children. It was just the two of us."

Stone stopped writing and looked at what appeared to be a truly hurt man. "I'm sorry, I know none of this is easy, but I'm trying to build a picture of how she lived so I can find the new factor in her life that brought us to this. I need to cut away at everything we know so we can find what we don't. If we remove everything, we know to be true in her life, then we can look at what is left. That will help lead us to who may have done this to her. One more question and I will let you go on, I'm sure you have a lot to still wrap your mind around. I hate to ask this, but why were you not living here with your wife?"

"We grew apart, me with my job. Whenever there was talk about kids we were never there at the same time. Something always came up for one or both of us."

"I really appreciate your help." Stone returned his notepad to its resting place. "You should get out of this Seattle cold."

"I'm used to it, but I would like to get away from here. I can't believe this is really happening. If that is the last of your questions, I'll be leaving now." The grief-stricken man walked to his car. He sat there for a moment before starting it and driving off.

"Did he tell you anything helpful?" Keith asked as they watched him drive away.

"Yes. She hated raisins."

RUFUS MONTGOMERY JR.

5

"BLOODY HELL!" SHE SHOUTED AS SHE FELL back into my arms. She pulled her bare feet out of a puddle of water. It rained the entire night before, but that is typical London weather.

"I got you." I place my arms around her trying to keep her from dropping everything she is holding. "Looks like you lost your shoe there."

"You bloody think?" She relaxed in my arms and laughed.

"Here, let me get that." I help her balance on one foot as I reach down to the puddle. I gently place my right hand under her foot to better help her from falling on her very nice ass. She is not what most people would consider a skinny woman, but she is someone you would say has a great body. She is dressed humble, yet sexy, and her hair is messy, but I can tell it started out much nicer before she left her flat. I pull her shoe from the puddle and empty the water from it. I watch her try to hide her blushing face. Here she is with her feet in my hand and her trying everything not to make eye contact with me. I look at her and shake the remaining water from her shoe, then to keep from bringing it to an end, I start blowing in it, attempting to dry it just a bit for her.

"You're having a bit of fun, aren't you?" she says as she finally allows me to see into her caramel-colored eyes.

"There you are," I reply, slipping on her left shoe.

"American?" she asks, noticing my accent.

That question always makes me laugh. "No, not exactly, but let's say yes for now."

"What does that even mean?" She says when she finally returns her feet to the ground.

"So, what do I call you when I'm sitting across from you having that drink you're going to let me buy you for saving the day?" I ask, changing the subject.

"Well, I can't very well say no, can I? You just had my foot in your hand." She frees up one of her hands by giving me everything she is holding in it. "Your mobile please." She wiggles her little fingers at me.

I reach into my jacket pocket, unlock my mobile and hand it to her.

"My friends call me Vicky. I don't know you, so you call me Miss."

"Who calls you Miss?" I ask as I notice she's left-handed.

"You do. You call me Miss. You seem a little dim. Are you sure you're not American?" We both laugh.

"I didn't say I wasn't," I say, "she now has my interest.

"The more you talk the more I hear a hint of something more. Are you here on holiday?"

"No, I'm here on business. I was taking a walk, looking for some inspiration before starting work." I give her just enough to see what she comes up with on her own. I am full from my last kill, so she will be entertaining between feedings.

"What do I call you?"

Well, this is something. I have no intentions of killing her, so it should be no problem telling her my real name. But, at the same time, I may just find someone in London that I do like and what then? I really like how she smiles, what could it hurt? Worst case is I kill her. She's standing there, smelling so yummy. I would just love to eat her, but that may have to wait until later. Or, maybe just a taste until it's time for more...

"You can call me Jason."

"When should I expect to hear from you, Jason?" she asks, reaching into my jacket pocket to put my mobile back before taking her bags from me.

"This is what I'll do..." I send her a quick text. She smiles as her mobile goes off in her purse.

"Who could look this beautiful stepping in a puddle?" I map her face with my eyes.

"Really?" She shakes her head. "You've already got my mobile number. You can save that for later. What did you text me, by the way?"

"Just something to keep me on your mind until we meet again." I reach over and grab a strand of hair hanging over her left eye and place it behind her ear. She smiles as she gently moves her face to touch her cheek against the back of my hand.

RUFUS MONTGOMERY JR.

"If I didn't know better, I would think you planned this. See you later."

I'm in no rush, so I watch her leave. What a morning. I could have walked with her. We were going the same direction, but timing is everything. You risk someone seeing too much. But it's not like someone is going to see it and yell, "Hey you're a killer!" Even though that would be a bit funny. Well, that one guy did wake up and the first thing he thought to say was, "Are you going to kill me?" What gave me away? Was it that he was sitting in his bathtub not able to move with his wrists slit? The right temperature of the water hides the correct time of death. Then there's the scheduled suicide text to your loved ones. Boy, do I love when technology does its job. That thin layer of ice that the mobile phone is floating on melts just right to destroy any evidence that may be left behind. Then there is always the question, "Why are you doing this?" I think that time I told him it was Thursday and I had time between appointments. The look on his face was priceless. I found myself just randomly laughing about that one for days. I'm sure some people thought I was crazy laughing aloud for what looked like no reason.

Dark Whisper: The Fire That Burns Within

I overheard what I could only assume was his wife talking about him in a nearby coffee shop about how the bastard killed himself and did not have the decency to hand write a suicide note. "Who sends a text? A group text nonetheless?" I thought I was going to piss myself before I could get my drink and get out of there. I should text her to see how she's doing. I ran into her a couple more times and did manage to get her mobile number. I figured why does the fun have to end now that he's dead. The woman found out about her husband's suicide via text. Who does that, for God's sake?

Anyway, enough reminiscing, I should head to my meeting. I am really not looking forward to sitting in a room filled with people trying to find the feelings in my art. How do I tell them my art is void of any feeling? I would, if at all possible, brutally murder them all and use the different shades in their blood to create my next painting. I would think nothing of it. Hey, look out! I grab this man by his shoulder and pull him back. Now this is altogether wrong. For one, I just hate unprepared human contact with anyone.

"Cheers, mate. I did not see that lorry coming. It would have bloody flattened me for sure." He hugged me and kissed

RUFUS MONTGOMERY JR.

my face ... MY FUCKING FACE! After saving this man's life all I can think about is killing his ass. Killing him right here, and when I'm all done kiss his dead face.

"Oh wow, you saved his life," I hear a woman's voice coming from behind me.

Her hands are on my hip. Is this another dead body? I turn to see what the fuck now. She stands there with black-rimmed glasses and the cutest smirk on her face. There's a look in her green eyes. It's almost like she sees me—like she's standing there looking at me with blood on my hands. For a moment, I stay trapped inside of my own head and her eyes at the same time. She stares into me, and what she sees is perfectly ok with her.

She pulls a pen out of her bag with some paper and writes something down. She leans in close and whispers, "It would have been much more fun if we could have watched him get hit by the lorry, but maybe on our second date. Call me." She reaches in my pocket, kisses my cheek, laughs, and walks away.

As I sit here in my meeting, I cannot stop thinking about her and how I couldn't tell how long her hair was due to how she had it up in a ponytail. I think of the gray skirt that hugged her ass as I watched her walk away, and the black and gray striped shirt that stopped right above the small of her back. The softest spot on a woman's body. I've always loved the reaction I get from kissing them there—the way they arch and shake, pulling away but then pushing back for more. I reach in my jacket hanging over the back of my chair and unfold it the note she put in my pocket. It simply says, "Come find me." Her number is written below it. I can't help but smile. "I can see myself killing her." I pull out my mobile to send her a text, but when I look, I already have a text from her.

> Let me know what time dinner is and maybe I'll let you hold my feet some more.
> —*Miss* (maybe you can call me Vicky later)

"Oh, boy."

"What was that, Jason? Is there something you're not liking so far?" My coordinator asks. "Did you want to add another painting with the five you're letting them sell? Are you sure you don't want to be named as the artist for your work?

They could sell for more if they had a face to go with the artwork."

"Absolutely not. When the others come in, remember I'm your assistant, but if you pull that "fetch your coffee" bull again, you're paying for your own room service the rest of your stay in London." I look up to make eye contact.

"Why is it that you don't stay at the same hotel as your assistant? I don't know where you're staying or how long you're going to be in the UK. Would it not be easier to work if I had more access to you? You disappeared for a week and then I get an email with my itinerary to London, and here we are."

"You already have more access to me than most people. The last time we stayed at the same hotel, it was weeks before you were willing to be in the same room with me, and another week before you could look me in the eyes."

"You're a bastard, you know that right?" she says.

I can't help but to laugh. "Yes, and I have the paperwork to prove it. When is a good time for me later? I need to be somewhere."

"You don't sleep, so what difference does it make?"

Dark Whisper: The Fire That Burns Within

"Good point. Let me send this text, then you can let the others in."

> Hello, Miss. 9:00 tonight. Let me know where. Drinks and late snacks. Look out for puddles. I'm not always going to be behind you.
> —Jason

"Okay, let them in." I get up and get ready to be her bitch. She walks out to the lobby of the building where they are waiting for her to give them the okay. It never ceases to amaze me what people will endure and or be subjected to at the promise of money. Here is the funny part; they're doing all of this for art painted by an artist they have never been in the same room with. Now, mind you, it did not start out that way at all. At first, we were the ones waiting in their lobby waiting to be asked in to hear if they would take just one of my paintings. But, after the one painting, they decided to take a chance on me. One painting sold for $100,000, then that man sold it to a collector shortly after for $500,000. That got their attention, and now they're waiting in their lobby to see which five of my paintings I'm going to let them make money on.

RUFUS MONTGOMERY JR.

Stacy comes back with the gallery curator, the owner and his assistant, and the specialists that will advise what five paintings the owner should spend his money on. If you were to ask me, I would tell you they were all shit. What I'm more interested in is if the curator is wearing underwear this time. I don't think everyone understands how much fun a woman is when she is in charge. Me just the lowly assistant of the assistant—man, I cannot get any lower than that. The first time she let me see her pussy, she thought she was doing me a favor. She just knew how pathetic my life had to be—getting coffee, carrying around boxes, and taking notes from meetings. She thinks I should be so fucking grateful for what she lets me do to her.

"Jason!" The owner comes over and shakes may hand. "How you doing, Laddie?"

It's always great to see this guy. He makes it easier than most to play human. Laddie is what my granddad used to call me before I had blood on my hands. He had a shit load of money, so he did not give a fuck what he said. A person like me can appreciate that. The best part is he hated my work and was really only there to see how much money we could make him and to see how much time I would have when I'm in London to help him get laid.

"How are you doing, sir? Very good to see you again." I prepare myself for what always comes next. He leans in for a hug. If I did not know better, I would think he was trying to fuck me. Is that his dick pressed on my leg?

"Come on, Jason, why are you still calling me sir? It's not like you've never seen my dick." Yes, and now it's on my leg.

"Sorry, Ben. I always forget about that dick thing. How have you been? Are we on for later this week?" I ask, still trying to get over the leg thing and hoping he is done hugging me.

"You're bloody right we're still on. That's the only thing that makes these hideous pictures worth my time. Now, speaking of them, where are they?" He finally lets me go.

"This way, Benjamin." Stacy points to fifteen paintings she has on display all around the room.

He walks right past her. "You can call me Mr. Nat, thank you. No need for the niceties. Just tell me how much of my money your wanker boss wants for this rubbish." I don a smile on my face long enough to receive a dirty look. I'm confused as to why he does not like her. She is a very beautiful woman.

RUFUS MONTGOMERY JR.

The specialists walk in, not even looking at Stacy and myself. They never say much to us if anything at all. They just come in and walk the room, putting different colored stickers on the frames. For the life of me, I still do not know what the fuck the colors mean.

"These are the ones we have to choose from this time around?" the curator asks as she walks past me just close enough for the back of her hands to graze my dick. There is a lot of dick action in this room this morning. "This is my kind of morning."

"What was that, Jason?"

"Nothing, Ben. Do you see any you like?"

"I can't say that I have, Laddie, but I do like how much money he makes me."

"I always forget to bring the portable display lights we have so we can have a better look at how they will look on the gallery floor." The curator walked out of the room to retrieve the lights.

"Would you help her with that, Jason?" Ben asks as he stands in front of a window looking out at the skyline.

"No problem, Ben." Stacy looks at me as to say, "don't leave me alone with this prick."

Dark Whisper: The Fire That Burns Within

I was not in her office long before I heard the door lock behind me. Now, here I am, the victim. She walks over to the couch, pulls her skirt up and bends over while looking back at me. "Can you get those for me?" I nervously walk over, trying to play my part in this game. I pull her underwear down slowly, and gently blow on her ass until I am low enough to be blowing on her wet pussy. Her back arches and the couch makes a sound that I can only assume were fingers clenching the leather. She puts one hand on her knee to stabilize herself. I lean in close enough to give it a soft kiss. She runs her hand up the inside of her thong and start rubbing on her swollen clit. My soft kisses turn into soft licking. She leans down even further and spreads her legs a little more giving me a better view of my early lunch. As she comes, I have to hold her legs to keep her from falling. I pull her closer so that I can be inside her feeling her pulsating as she climaxes on my tongue. I finally take her panties down past her ankles and under her heels and help her down to the couch. The tracks of her fingers when they slide down the black leather are still visible. She sits there flustered.

Looking down at her, I start unbuckling my pants. I pull them down just far enough to give her full access to my dick.

RUFUS MONTGOMERY JR.

She leans forward, and from the bottom of my shaft, she licks it all the way to the tip of my dick and puts her wet mouth up and over my head. She now once again has me at her mercy. I've got my dick in this woman's mouth and she still maintains her position. She never loses eye contact with me—even when she pulls back and opens her mouth just in time for me to see myself coming on her tongue. Being with her always fucks with my head because I still have no idea how I'm going to kill her yet, and how much I am going to miss her mouth.

"What the hell?" Stacy whispers as I walk past her with the lights I was sent to get. "What took you so long? You left me alone with this rich prick."

"What? I had to be very careful with the lights. They're fragile. That curator lady seems a bit mean, so I did not want to break her lights and piss her off, so I took my time."

"Jason, just get the lights up so they can pick the five they want so we can get the hell out of here."

"Yes, ma'am. I'll get right to it." I do just that and get those lights on my paintings. The curator walks in shortly after I do with more lights. I help her set up the remainder of them and the entire time I can still feel her mouth on me. Now, I just leave them to it and step off to the side and listen to everyone talk about me. I always wondered what people say when I'm not in the room, and this is truly a delight to witness.

I really get a kick out of Benjamin. I do not think he would be any different if he did know who I really was. It's probably the reason I like hanging out with him. Rarely do I get to be myself, which is funny because I have to claim to be someone else to do that. His assistant freaks me out. She wants to engage in small talk with me, and I am no good at that, except when the person is on my list. Lucky for her she is not on my list as of yet. She does not interest me much. I am pretty sure that I offend her every time I do talk to her. Don't get me wrong, it's not that she's not an attractive woman, but there is something about her that just bores me. That is what's keeping her safe. She entertains Ben and books us at the hottest VIP venues, so I'll keep her right where she is now.

Here she comes. Always with that folder pressed against her chest. She has her hair down for a change. Not bad. It makes her face look smaller than normal. She nixed the baggy dresses for a bit more of a form-fitting one—very nice for a plus sized woman. But still, what could she have to talk to me about?

RUFUS MONTGOMERY JR.

"Do you ever get tired of this part of the job?" she asks me, trying to open our annual small talk.

"What part of the job?" I ask.

"The part where everyone acts like the other person does not have something they want." She's now sparking an interest in me.

"Yes, it bores the hell out of me, but it is extremely entertaining." So far, so good. Maybe that's enough talk for now and she will move away.

"Me as well. How is he?" I could only assume she was speaking about the artist.

"Are you talking about the painter?"

"Yes. What kind of bloke is he?" she asks, looking up at me with her bright eyes.

"He is just like Ben called it. He is an asshole and not a joy to be around." Well, it's not like I'm lying. I've be called asshole so much that I'm sure I could get away with having it on my driver's license.

"Would you say you like working for him?" she asks. She looks at me, expecting me to do a magic trick now. I wanted to ask her if she wanted to see me make someone disappear. I did not answer, so she moved on to the next question. "What do you have planned for Mr. Nat and yourself this stay in London?" Now she's talking. I tried not to offend. I think I may have missed the mark.

"I have plans for he and I to change the lives and the vaginas of several women in your fair city. I think maybe I found a spot in Soho. But just in case, do you have any friends that know their way around ping pong balls and don't mind being naked around more than one man at a time? Don't worry, no one is going to touch her unless she asks us to."

Here we are again with her standing there like I had my dick pressed on her leg. I don't get it—she wanted to talk and now she's looking at me like my head just rotated. I give up on this small talk shit. "Okay, it's always nice talking to you. If you do think of a friend, Ben has my number." I pat her on the shoulder. I think that's right. "It looks like they're wrapping this up and Stacy is going to need my help putting the paintings away." I can never get away from her fast enough. Perfect timing on Stacy's part. She signaled for me to come over and that meant that this was almost over. Ben has the specialists leave to get some guys to help with the five paintings. Ben comes over to Stacy and me.

"I still have no idea why anyone would pay good money for this shit, but I am bloody glad that people love his work. For the life of me, I do not know why." He shakes Stacy's hand. "Jason it is always a pleasure to see you. I'll see you on Thursday. Tab will text you the details."

"Thank you, Ben. Don't forget to pack the bag with those hard-to-find items. And I would appreciate you keeping your dick out of my line of sight this time, please."

"I am looking forward to our outing, and as for that dick thing, no promises. That guy has a mind of his own." He leaves but not before checking out my assistance ass.

"I told you he likes you. Or at less he likes your ass."

"Will you shut up? Let's get out of here. Why do you like that guy so much? He hates you and your work."

"No, he hates my work and the guy he thinks is doing the painting. As for me, he can't get enough of me."

"Well, Jason, it looks to me like your friend, Mr. Nat, may want to fuck you. Maybe we can catch the next elevator."

She walks away. Who says something like that and just walks away?

"You see it too? I thought it was just me."

On the long ride down in the elevator, I remember the mobile number I have in my pocket. I pull it out and save it under "Kill or be Killed." For some reason, I thought it was fitting. What did she see when she looked at me with those haunting green eyes? How could she tell it was not in my nature to save that man? Did she somehow see that I would have rather seen him get taken apart by the lorry? That's all good and well, but what kind of fun can I get out of texting her and possibly meeting up with her?

"You going to do something with it?" Stacy asks, seeing me stare at my phone. Almost forgot she was in the lift with me. Okay, here I go.

> When's our second date?
> —Jason

Now all I can do is wait.

"Jason, what are you going to do for lunch?

RUFUS MONTGOMERY JR.

"I don't know. We both know I don't like food."

"Yes, that is why I'm asking. We both know if someone does not make sure you eat you won't."

And there's the setup. "Come on, Stacy, I ate you just fine and I don't remember you having to ask."

"Really, Jason? Why do you love bringing that up? Thought we said not to speak of it again." As the lift doors open to the lobby, we step off and walk to the exit. I look over and down at her. "If you saw your cum face and felt your legs closed around your head, trust me, you would bring it up too."

"That is such a messed-up thing to say, Jason, but somehow, it's flattering. Trust me, if the chance to come on your tongue presents itself again, I will take it. Are we going to have lunch, or are you going to keep talking shit about your mouth on my pussy?"

"That guy just heard you say the words mouth and pussy? God, that's great! That is why I keep you around. Can you say pussy again for me? I just love hearing you talk like that." She climbs into the car just right, so I can see the shape of her ass.

"The things that excite you are so weird. You getting in?"

"Oh, yes, boss lady, I will be getting in you."

"I think not. My shrink is still trying to talk me into quitting this job. She keeps saying something about you're most likely going to kill me one day."

Boy I need to make an appointment with this doctor. She sounds like she knows her shit. "Where are you taking me to eat?"

"There is this place I've tried, and the menu is pretty good. I am sure even with your eating habits, you will be able to find something on there. Since you did bring it up, I have always wanted to ask you."

"What is it that you want to know?" I ask her.

"With all the things I have personally seen that you are willing to do with your mouth, how is it you are the pickiest eater I've ever met?"

"Stacy, I will never tell."

"Okay," she says as she removes her Louboutin heels, revealing painted black toenails. Just how she knows I like them.

She slides to the edge of her set and puts her feet on my chest. I can't help but to think what happened to the sweet girl I gave this job to. I can only wait to see what she's up to. Stop her? Why? This could be fun. She continues to move her feet up my chest and lands them on my cheek. She puts her toes on my mouth, tracing my lips. She lifts her ass off the seat so that she can pull her dress up to give me the perfect view of her see-through panties. God, she has one of the most beautiful pussies I've ever seen—this is why I'm staying in a different hotel. The temptation is too much to bear. She runs her hands up her leg and pulls her panties to the side.

"Come get a snack before lunch, Jason. You have me wet and waiting. We both know you don't like leaving a lady like this."

As I grip her ass and pull her pussy into my mouth, I look up at her. "I thought I stopped being your bitch when we left the building?"

She looked down at me and grabbed the back of my head and put my mouth back on her. "You can be my bitch for just a little longer, now, eat up."

With the first touch of my mouth to her wet lips, I can feel her legs squeeze my head and her heels pushing on my back, pulling my face closer and deeper into her. Even with the privacy window up I'm sure that the driver can still hear her as she allows herself to forget where she is. She comes, not once, but over and over again until she is no longer pulling me close, but now she's pushing my head from her lap. I can feel a slight vibration in my jacket. I have just received a text. As I sit back in my seat, I still have a magnificent view of her pussy. I don't think she is ready to put it away. She still has her head thrown back and her legs open. As I pull out my phone, I lick what was left of Stacy off my lips.

> I see I didn't scare you away. That's good because I can see us having some fun.
> —Jason

> Not quite sure how much of me she saw, so I think I'll play it safe for now.
> —Miss

> Maybe we start with dinner before we get blood on our hands? Lol.
> —Jason

> That's fine with me. But next date we get our hands dirty.
> —*Miss*

"Now that you have had your first course, are you ready for fish and chips?" Stacy asks me.

"We both know we're not having fish and chips, but if you can find me some sushi, or some real seafood, that would be good."

"So be it," she says as she brings down the privacy window. "Excuse me, driver, do you know of a great seafood spot in London? My assistant is in the mood for something that use to be wet."

"It bloody well sounded like it," the driver says under his breath.

Now I know for sure he heard us. Oh, well. He could have seen everything, for all I care. "What you're saying is that you know a place?" I ask him as we exchange smiles.

"What are you two smiling about up there?" Stacy asks, getting suspicious.

"Just finding a seafood spot, Mum," the driver says, trying to keep from laughing.

"Who do you keep texting? Do you plan on leaving bodies all over London?"

When I hear her talk like that, I swear she knows. But how would she? And, if she does, why would she go out of her way to be alone with me every chance she gets? I say nothing and let her finish.

"Are you going to leave London covered with female bodies fucked and left wanting more?"

"No, that's Nat's thing. I just find him entertaining."

"I guess I can see that. Tell me something, what is behind your paintings? They seem very motivated by Poe without the darkness," She asks as she pulls back her jet-black hair that this London weather makes impossible to keep straight. The workday for us is over. She is becoming her real self.

"You know I've never been the one to talk much about my work. But, since I still have you on my breath, I will give you this one. As a kid, Poe's writing spoke loudly to me. The art in his writing, the dark in his words, and the beauty in the pictures his words painted. I was no good at writing, so I found the next best thing. I started painting and here we are. Can I ask you something, Stacy?"

"I don't see why not. After all, I do work for you."

"Why do you think Tab looks at me the way that she does? Do I freak her out that much?" By the blank look on her face, I think I may have asked a question that I should already know the answer to.

"Jason, you really don't know, do you? I think sometimes you don't hear what you are saying to people. I've known you for a while, and I use to think you just had a dark sense of humor, or you were really comfortable with me. The more I was around you, the more I notice you were not being cute and charming."

Wait! This is news to me. "You're saying I'm not charming?"

"Shut the hell up, Jason. You shouldn't be allowed to say the word. You say some shit sometimes that should not ever be said in public. Some of the things the poor girl has seen you and Benjamin do to people, I'm sure it has her a bit weary. Or it could be something else completely."

"You're going to make me ask? Fine. Stacy, what else could it possibly be?"

"If you must know, I catch her looking at your crotch all the time. I think she may just want to suck your dick. Driver!"

"We're nearly there, mum," he says.

As for what Stacy was saying, I could see it.

RUFUS MONTGOMERY JR.

"ARE YOU GOING TO TELL ME WHAT YOU WANT off the menu, because we both know you don't order for yourself if you don't have to."

Stacy knows me to well. Has the thought of holding her dead body in my arms ever crossed my mind? I would be lying if I said no. Then the thoughts of having to talk to people whom I would much rather be covered in their blood comes over me, and I'm glad I haven't killed her. Who else would tell the barista what I drink? If he gets it wrong, I end up following him home to peel the skin from his face for getting my drink wrong.

There is the way she looks at me. It is almost like she sees the animal I am and says, "Well, that's him." But could she be okay with the real me—the dark me that only shows himself at the end of my victims wretched lives? Or do I want her to know him? I would say no, not at the risk of losing her. To give up the thin tether of humanity she holds me to, would change everything. I would say she is pretty safe, but if I do not figure out what I want to eat soon, I will be the one in danger.

"Can I start you two out with a beverage?" the server asks as my blood runs cold. In the corner of my eye, I can see Indigo. I have never killed anyone with Indigo hair before. Her soft gray eyes reflex the color off her hair making them almost look deep blue. The skirt shows off her full legs. Nice and full, yet fit. I do not like a woman that feels she needs to be a size six. Though, she could use a little sun on those pasty white legs.

"Yes, and can you please take your hand off my friend's shoulder. He is really funny about human contact. But if you happen to feel his hand creep up that short skirt of yours, then it is open season. I mean, at that point, you can literally touch him anywhere, but we will have some water for now."

See? She even noticed the slight motion of me recoiling away when the server placed her hand on me. She even sometimes sees through my playing human.

"What would I do without you?"

"If you didn't have me, you would probably be put away for murdering someone for making that ridicules coffee drink you like the wrong way. Or be put away for kidnapping and torture of some unknowing young woman for placing her hands on you for no apparent reason."

I swear she knows something. "Yes, you hit the nail on the head. I would have most likely killed a lot of people if you were not here to save most of them. Can't let them all get away, can I? And about my hands up her skirt, did you want to take her home?"

"Let's get your order ready first, then we'll talk about what or whom we're going to do later."

I like how she thinks.

"I'm thinking the lobster and a salad. You can have whatever you want. I know how coming makes you hungry. In the car, I remember you saying something along those lines of "stay the fuck away from your pussy." What you had me do kind of went against that. rest assure that I have no problem with it."

"As long as my hand is on the back of your head, or your hands are away from me, and you let me have a mouth full of your dick, we are right where things need to be."

"You're saying as long as you are in control, things are as they should be?" Okay, I am pretty sure that is her foot on my crotch.

"Looks to me that you are not as slow as you would like us normal people to think. You're having lobster and I need a steak. See about that server. If we tip her good, maybe we can split her later."

"It can't be tonight, I have plans with someone that may or may not want to hurt me." Or she wants us to go on a killing spree.

"Whatever happened to that woman you met whose husband killed himself?"

It always cracks me up when someone says that about the poor bastard.

"She's doing well. I need to text or call her later." Special place in hell for me, I know it! But the time I spend with her is utterly delightful. I frequented that coffee shop day after day waiting for just the right time to step in and make a move. She'd go on about how happy they were, and how well things were going. She was confused as to why he would kill himself after just getting the job he wanted for years. Still, the bastard sent a text to his loved ones instead of a proper note. Who does such a thing? But I must ask myself; do I kill her as well? Or do I enjoy her like I have been?

"Where did you go just then, Jason? When your mind wonders off like that, the smile on your face creeps me out. What are you thinking about?"

My next possible victim and how I'm going to kill her. "My next painting. My mind runs away with me and takes me to my next vision I want to put on a canvas." One day I'm going to think that shit aloud and then she is going to know I'm really that bad. "It comes to me like a memory of something I have seen before—of a time I've spent somewhere doing something. Some places I have been, and some things I've seen, but most are of places and things I have never lived. I know it probably makes no sense to you, but it is how those ugly paintings come to be."

"That was beautiful."

"What the fuck! How long have you been standing there?" This server is pissing Stacy off. It's fun to watch. I think she may be getting a little like me and doesn't even know it.

"Pardon me. I didn't mean to listen in. It was like I was seeing him paint as he spoke those words. Let me go drop off this order and I will be right back to take yours."

"Ok, thank you. I'll make her be nice when you come back. I promise." To tell you the truth, I prefer her this way. This is when she is most attractive, and I can almost smell her pheromones rising off her skin. The night we first met, I was going to kill her. There was something about her skin that made me want to see it covered in blood. She had just started working for me. She was such a big part of my operation when everything was done through emails and some phone conversation. I was just trying her out to see if I could take it to the next level and sell more paintings and make more money. Don't get me wrong—I was not planning to kill her because she was doing a bad job—quite the opposite—she was great for my work and a great assistant to the point where I was not sure who was working for whom. It was one of our first business trips. No one knew she worked for me or even that we left the country. We did not take the same flight, nor did we check into the hotel together or pay for anything together, so there wasn't really anything tying us to each other.

RUFUS MONTGOMERY JR.

It was our first night in Italy. She was just a little thing—five feet if an inch. She had the greatest little curve in her back showing off her perfectly round ass The town we were in was both beautiful and quiet, and we wanted to eat somewhere with a view.

As we were walking to dinner at a highly recommended local spot, for some reason, this very bold man thought it wise to slide his hand across her ass. Stacy let into him with the strength of a thousand ancestors. Blood flowed up to her face and along her arms covering her skin with a sweet shade of red. It was like I was getting to see what I wanted without having to open her up to spill that sweet crimson.

That smell she gave off sealed her fate for that night, as well as the fate of the man who thought it was okay to touch someone under my care. I rushed over and saved him from her. Really, I was saving him for me. Now, his story I will say ended a bloody one and one I took immense pleasure in. When we finally arrived at the restaurant, she had calmed down a bit, but she wanted wine as fast as we could get it to the table. Drinking is not something I take lightly but I had one glass with her even though I was already intoxicated by her. The sun slowly came

Dark Whisper: The Fire That Burns Within

down over her left shoulder shining through her hair, and for a brief time, I forgot I was playing human. I gave her a look inside the artist and put the killer to bed.

She told me how she always dreamed of a job that would allow her to travel and do the things I've been able to make happen for her. She then started to enquire into me. The plan I put together in my mind was to lie my ass off, but when I opened my mouth, I heard the truth leaking out of me. She asked me what feeling comes over me when I paint. The truth is my art comes from the lack of feelings. If I were a writer, my writing would come from me giving it all up and letting the thoughts and the memories of the past me come forward and write their stories.

I told her how my paintings came from nowhere and everywhere I have never been and of a future that is not mine. In her eyes I saw confusion, and in the same eyes I could see her willingness to try and understand my madness. It's a look I have never seen in the eyes of anyone that has ever looked at me. At that time, and for the first time, I was glad I chose not to kill someone I liked. At that point, I could tell she was really the one for the job. I planned some things for the future of my work

RUFUS MONTGOMERY JR.

that most people would think me crazy for even saying it aloud, and I could tell she would find me just as crazy. Yet, she would go along for the ride if for no reason other than to see if we could pull it off with everyone watching. It was like I was a magician, and she was, well, my assistant. She found it so interesting that I was no good with people and despite all that, people wanted to be around me. She saw the way I read every one around—in a way to maneuver them into serving my purpose. She somehow knew all the right questions to ask. She started to love her job even more as she learned more about whom she was working for. Then she asked the big question that I had never thought of and had no answer until she asked. "Can you love anyone?" Her eyes were bright with anticipation, and her mind was open to anything that escaped pass my lips.

I sit back in my wicker chair breathing in the smooth, Italian air. I contemplated the question this woman had revealed to me—one that should be an easy to answer.

"Can you love?" she repeated, leaning in, waiting for the next words I spoke.

"No," I whispered.

Dark Whisper: The Fire That Burns Within

"I'm not sure if I've ever been loved. I have nothing to compare how love should be, and I'm not even sure I can give it to another. I have always been aware of my place in the lives of those around me, and I made sure to remain in my proper place." My voice returned to its earlier volume.

"How about your mother and father? Did you not feel love from them? They must have shown you love."

"What I was given may have, in a way, been defined as love from those looking in at what was taking place. I simply say it for what it was, and it came to be proven the older I became. I was being made into what they would eventually need me to be. To one, I was made into a knight—someone that would protect and serve to the point where I am incapable of letting them down. I see it as ingenious, really. You make someone into something that would go without food, sleep, or comfort to make sure you are taken care of. It is a hell of a thing to have achieved."

"And the other one?" She asked, now amazed at what she was hearing.

"The other is just as amazing. The other made it to where I would almost never need them, but still see them as someone you work your life to please and make proud as they do nothing to earn what you put at the center of the world you make. Now, are you ready to hear how I know I have never been loved?"

The look she dawned on her face earlier had changed to disbelief. Stalling, I offered to pour her another glass of wine.

"I'll pour it myself, just keep talking." She picked up the bottle and poured me a glass. "I think you need this more than I." We both laughed.

I nodded and wet my lips before taking a sip. "Well, this is how I know fully well and for sure that love did not play a part of what I was receiving from them. With all I have and am willing to do for them at any cost to myself, they would leave me to do for myself if for no other reason to give them time to get away."

She poured herself that last glass and wrapped her small hands around it the best she could. She brought it to her lips and leaned her head back as I watched her liberate the wine from its glass captor. As she returned it to the table, she made it clear what she thought. "That is fucked up!"

Dark Whisper: The Fire That Burns Within

I couldn't help but to laugh. "Yes," I said. "Yes, it is. But I am fine. It helped make me good at what I do."

"You think it helps with your painting?"

"My painting?" I was not referring to my work as an artist.

"Yes," she said.

Just like that, I remembered whom she still needed to know me as. "Yes, yes, it is why the me that only shows himself on canvas even exists. Guess that is one thing I can thank them for. Couldn't have done it without them."

For a moment, she made me think it was okay to be me with others looking. She looked into the mind of a killer and felt his pain and saw him as someone that puts beauty out for the world to see. A dark soul not even a mother could love. "Young lady, I think you have had enough to drink." I waved my hand to beckon for the check. "I should be getting you back to your room before it gets too late. We have an early start tomorrow. This will be your true interview. We get to see how well you are at being my voice."

"What do you mean by being your voice? Is that code for something?" she asked as I settled the check.

RUFUS MONTGOMERY JR.

"Come on, we're still on break and I do not like talking business while on break." I stood up and walked around to her chair. "I'll get more into it when I get you safely back to your room." I pulled out her seat and as she stood up, she lost her footing and fell back into my arms. I could not help but to laugh.

"You find that funny, do you? Well, good because you will be holding me up the rest of the way back to the hotel, funny man."

"Yes, ma'am. As you wish."

She wrapped her arms through mine and pulled herself in close to me. Little did she know that she was holding arms that have killed—that have held men so tight—I felt their bones break under the pressure. These hands have had the throats of women in them for no other reason but to squeeze the life from their bodies, yet these arms and hands are now dedicated to keeping her safe.

As we made our way back, the sun took its time setting, as if the day were not ready to end. I knew this was a day that would not come again for me, so I was okay with that. The new day will for sure burn off the small time I did spend almost being human. Was I being human, or was I showing her the killer that I truly am along with the bit of humanity I still possess? That was a question I would never be able to get the answer to.

"Do you ever wish there was someone to share all this with?"

"Excuse me?" I asked, not sure what she was saying.

"I know you said you haven't been loved or been in love, but do you not have the desire to have someone in your life. You know, someone to share all this with."

"Not really. I've grown used to being to myself and even in a room filled with people I am still truly alone." After saying that, she pulled me closer. There I was, trying to be okay with so much human contact. She went from being my next victim, to crossing lines that would get so many others killed. There she was, getting away with all of it. She amazed me.

"Well, Jason, I am here to keep you company until you get sick of me. Get used to being pulled outside your comfort zone."

I often wonder if that was what I was looking for, or was I just letting her live longer than expected?

RUFUS MONTGOMERY JR.

"So be it," I replied as I opened the door to the lobby. We walked to the lift. I pressed the button to call the lift down to us. I could not help but to wonder if she still needed my help to walk or was she just enjoying holding on to me at that point. When the doors opened, I let her in first, forcing her to let go. Standing next to her I leaned forward and pressed the fourth floor.

"Are you on the fourth floor as well?" she asked.

I smiled. "Yes, the room right across from yours."

"That is convenient." She looked across at my room door.

Red light, *click*. Red light, *click*. "Would you like me to open that for you? Looks to me like you're having trouble."

"Yes, thank you, that would be great. Don't know what is wrong with it. Had no problems with it when I checked in. Speaking of checking in, I didn't see you when I was checking in." Stacy was still standing very close to me as I opened her door with ease.

"I've been here for two days now. I was probably out when you came in. How did you like the car that you arranged to be picked up in?"

"I don't remember doing that."

I helped her into her room. "That's part of what we need to go over. May I come in?" I asked, like a vampire waiting for an invitation.

"Of course, you may. I am dying to hear what we are getting into tomorrow," she said, standing there holding the door open, her eyes bright with anticipation. A goofy smile spread across her face. I go over to a single chair with its back to the window and the couch to my right. Eliminating the possibility of her sitting too close. She kicks off her shoes as she disappears into the bedroom.

"I'll be right out, just going to use the little girls room."

"I think this room is nicer than mine." I took a good look around.

"Good," she shouted. "Because by the sound of things, I paid for it."

As she came back into the room, I noticed she had put her hair up, exposing that lovely neck of hers. That neck I had fully planned to partake in that night. She walked over to the couch and threw herself down, crossing her legs with no regards to the fact that I could see everything from where I was sitting—

pink trimmed panties with black lace. The pink was see-through enough that I could tell she waxed for her trip to Italy. The aroma she gave off in the marketplace was still there strong as ever and just as yummy. I remembered why the sight of her neck brought different feelings out of me. I adjusted myself in my seat. "Now as for tomorrow..." I kept eye contact, trying to avoid looking at her partly exposed vagina. "It is going to be very important for them to see you as the person in charge of this sale. They need to see me as nothing more than your assistant. The least attention they pay to me, the better."

As she sat there still a little buzzed, trying to take in all that I was telling her, I couldn't fight back the desire to see her bleed, but there was something about her that made her a great fit for what I needed her for—to make me invisible.

"Okay, so what it sounds like to me is you want me to have everyone believe that I'm in charge of the deals that we will be making tomorrow?" Her feet were back on the floor, taking away the view I had of her soft parts.

"Yes, and not just tomorrow. What I've described to you is what you have been hired for." At that point, I expected her to see me as the crazy person I clearly am, but to my surprise, it seemed to get her excited. Again, she asked all the right questions.

"How am I to know what those drawings are worth?"

That question got me. I had to stop and think what they were worth to me. Then I had the answer. "They are worth nothing to me, so you really can't go wrong, but to motivate you, your salary will be what the second most expensive painting goes for." When she heard that, she looked at me like I had just bought her a puppy.

"You have to be kidding me. I know what your paintings could go for." She threw herself back on to the couch.

"Yes, and this time you get that great first paycheck. If you do as good as I am sure you will do, who knows what will be waiting for you next. Make me invisible tomorrow and sell some paintings for a lot of money. It's late, and you need to get some sleep." I got up and walked to the door with her close behind me. I turned to say goodnight, just to find her almost pressed against me, still a little drunk. "Well, goodnight, see you at breakfast."

I quickly left the room. Unbeknownst to her, she had put me in a mood, and since she was given a stay of execution, there

RUFUS MONTGOMERY JR.

were not a lot of choices left. That's when I reached into my pocket and found the wallet that I lifted off that piece of shit that was pulling on Stacy earlier at the market. It was still early in the evening, so I went to my room and pulled out something I brought with me in case of such an occasion. I memorized his home address, which could not be far from the market since he was walking and not driving. I cleaned his wallet of all traces of me and placed it in a sealed bag and returned it to where he was last seen hoping someone would find it, and he would come back looking for it.

In the meantime, I went to his house, and made myself familiar with the area. He lived in a lovely two-story villa, and from what I could tell, he lived alone. I saw no reason not to let myself in and take a little look around. I could tell that he did a bit of drinking by the collection of empty wine bottles he had. He seemed to live very well, despite his dinking. Only question was how he was going to die. As I was leaving, I walked past a beautiful knife set he had sitting on the kitchen counter. Call me crazy, but it said my name. The first thing I thought wasn't "what the fuck is this knife set doing speaking," no, what I thought was how does this thing know my name, and that this

Italian knife set speaks perfect English. I took one of the smaller knives and left. It was pretty dark out and I was just taking it all in as I did what I did best—painting a picture of the death of someone that had no idea that they were dead. Finally, he came home, walking through the poorly lit alley that I took on my way to his villa.

Just like I expected, he went through his wallet, making sure there was nothing missing. What have I already said? Pay attention to what is going on around you, because you never know when I will be waiting somewhere you least expect ... to find me with a knife from your kitchen ready to slowly slide it into that sweet spot in your neck. That spot keeps you from screaming out because every time you try to scream blood rushes into your lungs making you feel like you're drowning. As you are on your knees holding the knife in, looking up at me unable to ask me why I am doing this, I watch you trying to hold on to what little air you can.

I took his wallet, removed what money he had, and after watching his last breath bubble from his neck, I walked to a nearby church and made a deposit in the collection box before going back to the hotel. I changed and went to the gym. I was still pretty worked up, so I put in a quick hour. The next morning, Stacy and I went to our first meeting. I sat there, invisible, as she sold painting after painting and even set us up for a future gallery show. I am sure she knew from the homework she did on me, I was not known to do shows.

When we got in the car after the meeting, I asked her what's up with the show. She simply smiled, and said she got carried away. I couldn't do anything but laugh.

"Do I have the job?"

"Really? At one point in the meeting, I was worried you would fire me because I wasn't moving fast enough. The job is yours. You made a lot of money today, so you can buy me dinner tonight." I'd already killed for her, so I may as well have kept her around.

7

"I REALLY HATE WHEN YOU GO AWAY LIKE that. It's like I'm here alone." Stacy's voice pulls me back from thought. "Are you off painting in your head or something?"

"Something like that." It's art, but it's not painting. "See if the fish they have comes with the face still on it."

"Really, Jason? How often do they have fish with the fucking face on it when we go anywhere? Yet you always make me ask. I'm starting to think you just like the look they give me when I ask. If they don't, then what do you want?"

She's right. I love the look they give when she asks for a fish with the head still on it. That shit is great. "If not, just get me sushi with a side of celery and steamed oysters for us both."

She sits there and gives me the same look she gives when she wants to know what my plans are for later, if we will be working again tomorrow, or will she be spending the rest of our stay in London ordering fish with a face for me. What will I do? Fuck with her head. "Are we taking her home?"

"Who?" She looks around.

"The server with the great ass. She clearly likes you, and I think she can smell your pussy on my breath." I may have said that a little loud. The sweet old lady at the other table just smiled at me.

"Will you keep it down, please?"

You would think she was used to me by now. Stacy is still a little shy when it comes to some things.

"I am not a lesbian. I don't like girls. I've told you that."

I smile. "But there was that one time when—"

"We said we would never speak of that." Her face turns red as a tomato as she tries to hold back a smile.

I love that look on her face every time I bring it up.

"Have you both decided what you want?"

Now the fun begins.

"Yes," Stacy replies. "We're going to have the steamed oysters to start with. Then, I will have the roasted chicken with a side of veggies."

I give her my best puppy dog look, but it doesn't bloody work.

"As for him, he will have the sushi with a side of celery." She gives me her famous "fuck you" look—a look I get far too often. I honestly can't blame her, though.

"Will that be all?" The pretty little server has no idea what game she's in the middle of. I could leave things alone, but if any of you know anyone like me, you know some shit is about to fall out of my mouth.

"Yes, one more thing. Before you came back, my lunch companion and I were having a discussion, and she is a bit shy, so I'll ask. Now, I know from experience my friend here has the loveliest little clit you will ever see."

"Jason!"

"No, it's okay, Stacy, I've got this. Anyway, we were wondering if by any chance you would like to go at that magnificent clit? I assure you the sound she makes when she comes will be worth it."

Not sure what to say, the server sticks to her script. "I will go put your orders in." She quickly takes her leave from our table. Now, I have a clear view of the sweet little old lady. I give her a wink.

"Jason, you really are an ass," Stacy says as she sees me making nice with the sweet senior from the other table.

"Say what you want, but I guarantee her husband is getting lucky tonight. There will be some old lady face-sitting tonight for that guy." I truly do not know why she puts up with me.

"Not that. You now have the server thinking I want to have sex with her."

"You?" Stacy clearly doesn't get my plan. "Sex with you? You've got it all wrong. We are fucking her in your hotel room. Not tonight, because I have a thing, but before we leave this country, your clit is going in her mouth, count on that."

Stacy can't hold her little squeak back anymore. Even though I am a bit difficult to maintain, I always take care of her, and make sure she has a good time and does things she only thought she would read about in books. I am that devil on her shoulder that takes the blame for all the bad she has found herself in the middle of since she started working for me. I 'm sure you're asking yourself how much Stacy really knows about

Dark Whisper: The Fire That Burns Within

what I do when I'm left to myself. Keep up and you may see what this sweet innocent young lady knows, or maybe she has no idea and just sees me for the eccentric artist that I am. Because I am very much that as well.

"Oh, look, our food is here, and it all looks so good. Don't you think so, Stacy?" I ask, knowing how much trouble I'm in already. Oh, well. I'm going all in.

"Yes, Jason, it all looks very good." As the server starts to walk away, Stacy grabs her hand. "Would you like to know what else looks very yummy?"

I wipe the water I managed to spit down the front of my shirt. "What the hell, woman? Are you trying to drown me? What was that?"

"I can't let you have all the fun. It is my pussy you're putting up as collateral, plus if you do drown, maybe you will shut the hell up." I can't help but to agree with her.

"Good point. That's why you make the big bucks." I have to say, I'm clearly not a fan of humans, but I am fond of the one sitting across from me. She understands my need to be seen and still remain invisible and be so willing to do her part to keep me that way. Sure, the money is good, and I'm sure was her

RUFUS MONTGOMERY JR.

motivation to take the job, at first. Now, it seems to be more than just a job to her—she does much more than the job requires.

I sit across from her watching her eat like we have done so many times before, but the desire to see her in pain has not gone away. Something I still do not fully understand is the desire to inflict pain so much different from wanting to bring about pleasure to the same person.

Let's take a man interested in having sex with a woman; does he worry that he is going to hurt her, or does he brag about how much damage he is going to do to the pussy. When she bends over on all fours with her sweet ass up in that perfect position—we all know the one—the only thing you have to do is walk right into her. First you slide your dick into her wet, welcoming vagina, and you feel her tense up and you hear that moan of pain as you feel the sheets shift under you as she grips the bed. That was just the tip. Now do you (A) pull your dick out and say sorry I didn't mean to hurt you, or do you (B) smile and slide the rest of you right into her? I know what I do. I keep going, but I don't put it all in, not just yet. What I do is get her nice and used to some of what I have waiting for her. It starts to feel good. As she loosens, her moans of pain turn into moans of pleasure and then she comes. Her pussy pulses around my dick as I watch her ass vibrate out of control. That's when I know it's time. I put my hand on her waist right where her ass stops and pull her on to the rest of my dick, watching as everything changes for her. Her back curves, and her head falls back. She doesn't just grip the sheets—she pulls it so hard the mattress comes up. I give her a full thrust and keep the same rhythm until she can't decide if it's pain or pleasure. I can't distinguish the two from her screams. But I take her pushing her ass back on me is the clue that she is having as much fun as I am. I come just in time to feel her come again and watch as her body goes limp, and she slides off my dick and lies down. I stay for a moment, as she slowly closes back up.

Ask any guy when his dick the hardest, and he will say it is right before sex, or during sex when you hear her moan with pain and pleasure. Hey, maybe it's just me. Maybe I'm the only sick fuck out here, but I am okay with that.

"How's your sushi?" Stacy asks softly.

"It's very good, thank you," I reply.

"Are you doing that thing you do?" Stacy asks.

RUFUS MONTGOMERY JR.

The thing she is referring to is how I sit and observe the people around me. To be honest, even with a plate of food right in front of me, I'm still looking to feed a different hunger.

A smile creeps across my face.

Stacy starts looking around the restaurant. "Who are we looking at, and what's going on?"

I motion to my left to a couple by the window close to the entrance. "Those two over there are on a first date."

"How can you tell?" she asks as she turns slightly to get a better look.

I lean forward. "I thought you would never ask. Look how he is leaning in at her every chance he gets. He is testing how close she will let him get to her. Not only that, but he's also trying to imagine how his dick is going to look in her mouth."

"Jason, shut the fuck up. How could you even know that?"

"Stacy, which one is it? Shut the fuck up or tell you?" She pinches the back of my hand. "Okay, tell you. I will. Do you ever notice on a first date a guy tries to be funny?" She nods, hanging on the words that are not yet out of my mouth. "Well, when someone hears something funny, they laugh, and when most people laugh, they throw their heads back and open what?"

I watch as the light turns on in her eyes and she thinks back to every date she has ever been on. "I see you get what I'm saying by the look on your face. Not to mention, no matter how much time you take getting ready and trying to look your best, the first thing a guy thinks when he sees what you are wearing is how much work it will be to take it off. If you come out in a dress, he is looking to see if it needs to go over your head or does it fall right off. Let's say you happen to have on a skirt. He is now trying to see if it's just a zipper or buttons. To find that out he does a certain move."

"What move?" Stacy asks, dying to know what this move is.

"I'm sure you've had this happen to you before. It's when a guy takes every chance he gets to place his hand on your waist. He is feeling to see where the zipper, button, and or hook may be."

She is thinking now. I know because she has that look on her face. This is never good for me from what I have seen, so I wait. Finally, she puts it all together.

"That first night in Italy, you were very funny. Were you picturing your dick in my mouth?"

I have a choice. I can tell her I was looking at her neck thinking about where to place my hand to get the best results of slowing her breathing, but I think that would make our relationship a bit awkward, so I give her the best possible answer.

"Yes, I could not stop thinking how great your lips would look on my dick." I smile my famous smile.

"You're an ass," she says as she kicks me under the table. "How about what I was wearing?"

I quickly reply, "Dress with a zip down the left side, over the head if you want but faster if you drop it." The look on her face was priceless. "But that boy is fucked anyway."

"Why do you say that?"

"She is wearing pants." We both laugh.

"Is everything okay over here?" the server asks nervously.

"We are good, and we are ready for the bill now please. Oh, and give us their bill as well." I look to the sweet old couple as I gently touch the back of her hand. I could feel little goose bumps raise, and the warmth of blood rushing through her. She backs away, bumping into the table behind her.

"Sorry," she whispers.

I keep eye contact with her the entire time. You would think a man like myself, with so much to hide, would avoid something like eye contact. It's like they say, "The eyes are the gateway to the soul." Fucking good thing I don't have one.

"Why are you doing that thing? Don't tell me you're still working on her, Jason. I am pretty sure she is afraid of the both of us. Don't give me that look. That look means shit is about to fly."

"Ten thousand says she is into us both." I have to make it good because I know how much Stacy loves a good bet.

"After that shit you pulled, ten thousand and I'll suck your dick whenever and wherever. Call it a free one on me."

"Trust me, I'm going to get it on you. Here she comes, bets are closed, and we say nothing. At this point, it is what it is."

She stops, and whispers to the nice old lady and points over to Stacy and me. The nice lady laughs and her and her husband wave and say thank you. The server slowly walks over with an unsure look on her face, making a clear effort not to look at me. She quickly places down the bill in front of me.

"I hope you two enjoyed your meal."

Before we could reply she rushes off.

"See, just terrified. She couldn't get away from us fast enough," Stacy says.

Even though Stacy keeps our card we use to pay for expenses, the check always comes to me.

"How does it look?" she asks.

I shake my head in disappointment. "Looks like ten thousand to me."

"You're the ass that wanted to bet. Give me the check so I can pay it and get out of here so that poor girl can do her job. We had our fun with her."

I slide the black folder across the table.

"FUCK." she whispers.

"That's right," I reply. "Ten Thousand and that whenever blow job. Make sure you don't lose that number. Know what, let me save it too in case you want to waste the chance of a strange tongue on your clit. God, it feels good to be right."

She puts the card away, pulls out pounds and pays in cash. "What?" She grabs her things and starts off.

"I don't want to be here when she gets back. You're setting this one up, Jason."

I get up, get my jacket, and follow like a good boy. "Yes mum," I say loud enough to be heard by everyone in the restaurant. My last poke at her as I make my big finish. She gives as good as she takes.

"Shut the fuck up, Jason," she says, no longer being able to hold back a smile and a little laugh.

We manage to make it out of the restaurant without her taking a steak knife to me, so I call it a good lunch. I walk her over to the car and signal to the driver that I have the door. It's just a thing I like doing for her. Before she climbs in, I pull her close and kiss her on the forehead.

"Are you not coming with me?" Stacy looks at me with her arms tight around me.

"No. I'm going to find another way." Those eyes are looking through me.

"Does it have anything to do with the text you've been getting?"

RUFUS MONTGOMERY JR.

I avoid the question. "Do we have another thing tomorrow?" Without her, I would not make it to anything that I didn't set up myself.

She shakes her head and loosens her grip. "Yes. We meet up with Ben at the gallery to take a look at the layout. Before you ask, yes, you need to be there." She climbs into the car. Her eyes worry me because they look like the eyes of someone that's in love with me. Not much scares me, but those eyes scare me more than the first time I knew for sure I was the killer you see today. I play human for her and lean down and softly kiss her lips. "Yes. I will be careful. I'll see you at breakfast."

Dark Whisper: The Fire That Burns Within

EVERY TIME OF DAY HAS A HEARTBEAT.
After lunchtime, it's like, everyone is on the move and watching them all is like the opposite of those animal shows. But I am the animal watching the humans in their habitat. Some of them leave work—others leave for work on the late shift—some are just returning to work from lunch. The human chatter taking place is always a fun thing to sit and listen to. It's about all things and nothing at the same time. The small talk is something I have yet to master myself. I think it may come from the fact that I am always so interested in the workings of the human mind; they think of the weather. What I have mastered is pulling apart small talk and getting to the meat of the victim I'm talking to. Wait. I said victim. What I meant was person. Not everyone is a victim, but the line between the two is very thin.

RUFUS MONTGOMERY JR.

As I was saying, people mostly small talk about the safest things they know. The weather, TV shows, or the news. These are all safe things—things others most likely know something about so to keep the small talk going. I play the game we call "small talk" with the humans till it's time to play my own game called "let's see what's really on your mind." At first, I let something personal slip about myself—true or not, it does not matter, because it is just to trick them into safety. In order for them not to feel left out, you've got to say something about yourself.

What do most people want more than anything? To be listened to and to feel like they are special and everything about them is important. I am there to make them feel just that about themselves. I give them my undivided attention and let them tell me everything I could ever want to know about them. I've had it work so well in the past that I had a woman tell a table filled with strangers that her and her boyfriend did not use condoms and just comes on her face. The look on everyone's face was the greatest thing I had ever seen. The best part was I had her feeling so comfortable that she didn't think twice about what she was saying. I had to let her live. The embarrassing look on her

Dark Whisper: The Fire That Burns Within

face was the same face of people that realize that I'm really about to kill them.

In a nutshell, I get people to say the quiet part out loud.

London has to be one of my favorite cities. The CC cameras everywhere help to keep an animal like myself playing nice with the humans. Don't get me wrong, it doesn't stop me from partaking in the goods that this city has to offer, but it does give me the chance to see how good I really am at what I do. Not riding with Stacy and walking back to my hotel was to pull away from the humanity she found a way to pull out of me. I tell myself she is a necessary part of my life to keep things going, but I lie better to you guys than I do to myself, so I try to take her in small dosages. Also, sometimes I can see me rubbing off on her, and I can't have that happen. I can see her killing a lot of people just because, and as fun at that would be to watch, I can't have that going on. There have been times when I thought she was ready to kill someone, but the me that actually kills was able to calm her down. I think it's only fair she has kept me from killing a number of people over the years.

As I approach the entrance to the train station, I can feel the heat climbing from underground like breath escaping the city. I enter the warmth of the tube. You find all kinds under here, or maybe even some like me. I look around trying to see if I run across a familiar face or two. Stepping on to the tube, the first thing I do is scan, starting with the people closest to me, then all the way to the back as far as I can see. The businessman trying to act as if he did not belong in this metal beast like the rest of us gets my attention right away. As we know my attention is something most people don't live long after getting. He looks up briefly and sees me. It must be the suit, tie, and the shiny shoes that I'm wearing that makes him feel like he and I are one in the same. He makes eye contact with me. God, he is doing everything wrong this evening. The sun is going down, and it has been some time since I've listened to that dark whisper, or just listened to myself for that matter.

Playing human has never been easy or fun for me, but most times necessary. I notice a wedding ring. Maybe I can find other entertainment with him. I may just let him live. Making my way over to where he has his briefcase, I proudly sit next to him.

There is a roughly dressed girl sitting across from him. She may be twenty-one, twenty-two, wearing shorts barely covering her ass. I would say she is not wearing panties. Why do

Dark Whisper: The Fire That Burns Within

I think that? Well, before my friend there with the lovely briefcase noticed that I stepped onto the scene, I noticed a few things about him. At first glance it looks as if he is reading the paper and trying not to make contact with the people around him.

If you know what you are looking for, you will see that behind his tilted glasses, his eyes are fixed on her knees waiting for them to open again. The tube does a thing where it shifts and bounces just right, making most people feel like they were going to be tossed from their seat. When that happens, she throws her legs open, planting her feet hard and wide on the floor of the metal serpent dragging us beneath the city. When that happens, he gets a good long look at where babies come from. Not saying that she has any kids, but you know what I mean. I have to give it to him—he picked a good seat. He quickly moves his briefcase from the seat, freeing it up to allow me to sit down. Unknowing to him, he just let the devil in the door.

"Cheers," I say as I sit down.

"Now worries, mate," he replies, still focused on his prize.

RUFUS MONTGOMERY JR.

I can have fun with this guy if I get her where I want her. She is not a modest girl, and if given the right motivation, she will knowingly give him what he is working so hard to get a glimpse at. I need to work fast, there aren't many stops until I get to mine, and I have no idea where they are going.

I begin, "Very nice briefcase."

"Cheers," he says with pride in his voice as if I just told him he had a cute kid or something. And they say something is wrong with me.

"What do you do for a living that allows you to afford such a case?" I keep the compliments coming to help him open up.

"I work in pharmaceuticals. I do the marketing for up-and-coming drugs." He is enjoying the bump and shift that just started.

"Would you like me to help you with that?" I whisper.

He turns to me, surprised but not very embarrassed.

Leaning over he whispers, "You mean help with her?"

I'm a little shocked. This fucker is not even trying to deny that he is looking at this girl's pussy. Who the fuck am I sitting next to? "Yes," I reply. "What would you say if I could get her to give you a better look? Would you go for that?"

"I would bloody love to see you pull that off. You would be some fucking bloke if you could do that," he says, now getting too close to me.

If he gets any closer, I'm just going to kill his ass on the next stop.

"Okay, watch this," I say, noticing that we are coming up to a tunnel. According to the announcement, my stop is coming up shortly after, so I need to get this done quickly. I walk to an empty seat next to her. I can see the excitement in his face just as we enter the tunnel. I lean over and work my magic before we clear the darkness. Her eyes are now fixed on him, and he is not sure how to react. I put my hand on her right knee and slowly pull them apart as she and I watch the anticipation on this fucker's face. She runs her left hand up her inner thigh to where little to nothing covers her vagina. She pulls what little that was still covering it to the side and shows him all she can without actually taking her shorts off. The tube comes to a stop, and I get up.

RUFUS MONTGOMERY JR.

Tapping him on his shoulder, I become his dark whisper and say, "You have fun now." I step off, disappointed that I won't get to see what happens when she asks for the thousand pounds, I told her he was going to give her for a good look at her pussy. Oh, well. I guess I can't win them all. Plus, I have a date to get ready for.

"Thank you," I say to the door attendant as I walk past him and think to myself if this is necessary. Really, there is a man who stands there and opens the door for people too lazy or rich to open doors for themselves. Take the piece of shit that walked in right behind me. He didn't even have the decency to say cheers or thank you.

"Excuse me," I say to him. I turn as if I've forgotten something, and bump into him. I pat him down and try to straighten him back out. I walk to the door attendant with my wallet in my hand, and wave to get his attention.

"I forgot to tip you for a job well done." I pull out what has to be about four to five hundred pounds. I guess I would know exactly how much I have if it were really my wallet.

"Cheers, mate," he says as I close his gloved hands around the thick role of money. "Are you sure?" he asks.

"Yes!" I shout back. "It was nothing. Thanks again for doing such an excellent job." Seeing what I did, the rich shits that would normally pass him as if the door magically opened itself take money out and tip him as well. We all know rich people hate to look like they have less to give then the next rich shit. I use a napkin I have in my pocket to wipe off the wallet. As I get on the lift, I drop it into the waste bin wrapped in that napkin. Not like he will miss that money. Seems like he had more money than he knew what to do with.

As a smile creeps across my face, I feel the lift jerk and go up to my floor. Only thing that would have made that better is if I had been able to kill that man right there in the lobby. With everyone just looking on thinking, "What the fuck?" I will get him next time. The loud ding fills the metal box. Needless to say, I hate sharing the lift. Why do people feel the need to say something to you? Get on, take the ride, and get the fuck off. I don't care where you have been or where you're going. Asking me the wrong question could very well get your body hidden. I haven't gotten far when the door opens on the second floor.

"Would be my luck," she says as she awkwardly hands me some of her luggage. "Got all the way to the wrong room before seeing it was a five and not a two. You would bloody think I couldn't count."

What in the hell is going on here?

"Can you press five for me, please?" she asks me.

Still not sure what's going on, I reach over and hit the five. I want to know why one person needs this much stuff. Only two of us in the lift and there is nowhere to move away from her.

She looks around. "This lift is so small"

No, bitch, you just got too much shit. "Yes, too small." I reply and hit that five again. "And slow," I add. She stands there holding the doors open with her feet. Now I know I am being fucked with. I still gather her things and follow her down the hall. What am I doing? She could be a killer taking me to her kill room. Wait, why have I never thought of this. This would work. Shit, it's working on me, and I should know better.

She stops in front of a room, looks at the number on the door, to the papers in her hand, then at the door again. "I think this is me."

"Try the key," I suggest.

"What?" She looks at me.

I smile, still playing human. "Try the key. If this is your room, your key will open it."

"Oh, yeah, the key. Good one," she replies, excited.

It opens right up. This is her room, and this is almost over. She drops the bags she's holding right at the door inside her room. I proceed to pull what I had of her things in when I feel her small hand on my chest.

"Just a minute, handsome. I don't know you. You could be a killer for all I know. I'm not letting you into my room. This is as far as you go." She liberates her bags from my hands and rolls them into her room.

The look on her face is as if to ask me what I was thinking. The look of confusion on my face as the door slowly closes must be something to see. It feels like I'm moving in slow motion as I walk back to the lift.

"Hey!" she shouts at me, running down the hall.

I can only think I should move faster. I turn in time to have her throw her arms around me. "Thank you." She gives me a kiss on the check and slips a piece of paper in my hand. "Let me get you a drink to thank you." She runs back to her room.

RUFUS MONTGOMERY JR.

I am still not sure I'm safe around her. I finally make it to my room three floors up. I even look behind me to make sure she's not there. I have always attracted some of the strangest people. As I take off my jacket, my phone goes off.

```
Hope you didn't forget me already.
—Vicky
```

```
Not at all. In fact, I was just thinking
about you.
—Jason
```

```
What were you thinking about me?
—Vicky
```

```
Was hoping you managed to keep from stepping
in puddles.
—Jason
```

```
Is that it?
—Vicky
```

Dark Whisper: The Fire That Burns Within

No. I was also hoping I would get to see you again soon.
—Jason

That's better. I was starting to think you lost your charm. Since I know London better, should I come to you?
—Vicky

I know London pretty well, so I will meet you wherever you would like. Just give me a time and place.
—Jason

Sounds good to me. Do not have a place in mind just yet. I'm going to have a bath and think on it.
—Vicky

Just let me know. I will get ready.
—Jason

RUFUS MONTGOMERY JR.

Now, what to wear? This is not a night for maroon. I do not even know if I like her or not. I'm thinking comfortable and laid back. Only other thing is am I going as Jason tonight, or the other guy. Definitely Jason. That other guy is a killer. I can't wait to get out of this suit, just can't get used to having to dress like this. This is a night to be comfortable, so jeans and a button up it is. The hardest question now is what underwear to choose. Maybe I wear none at all. As I walk past the mirror on the wall, I'm startled by my reflection. Spending time being someone else, you build a different outer look that you start seeing yourself as. You try to abandon things that tie you back to the real you. Your walk, the way you talk—all of it is different. It has to be. You even refrain from using words that the other you may use. Your mannerisms, right down to your laugh gets changed to fit this new person that you have made to hide the killer you truly are. One of you may speak with your hands, while the other has his hands in his pocket. One of us bites his lip when he gets nervous, whereas the other guy looks at everyone like they are naked. Then it comes down to that time someone sees the one who plans to watch the life leave his or her body. Let us just say that there is no one that is around to share that secret with

Dark Whisper: The Fire That Burns Within

others, and sometimes I have to ask myself who was that who grew up in my place. You may wonder what that means. Let me try and explain. Imagine not being a part of your own childhood. You are there, of course, but you have step out of who and what you are. Most people like me can trace who they are because of some childhood trauma such as a run-in with a priest or a touchy friend of the family, or something of that nature. Well, not me. I was the light of my grandmother's eyes, and from her I learned how to play human. To this day, I am who I am to protect her from the grandson she did not deserve to have. I tried to be the perfect grandson. From bringing home good grades to singing in church, I tried until it was time to cause animals pain just so I could watch them suffer. I did thinks like pinning a snake in an ant's nest to watch it be slowly devoured. I would have to say my favorite was when I found a large white block that I thought was chalk but turned out to be a flammable powder. I set a rat on fire and watched as it ran down the street. Here I am getting distracted, thinking about the good ole times. I should be standing here trying to decide whom Vicky is going to meet tonight. It's so much easier to just be myself. That settles it. She gets to play with me tonight. I hope she is open-minded.

RUFUS MONTGOMERY JR.

9

"YOU'RE TELLING ME YOU COULD NOT FIND any evidence of anyone else in that house but her?" A raised voice cut through the quiet of the room. "Is there anything you can tell me that could shine a light on anything?" Silence. "You think telling me that other than her body in the room there wasn't any evidence that she was in the room either? That is what you thought would help? I'll be right down." The desk shook from the phone being hung up.

Stone flung the chair back as he stood up. He turned to start his march on the morgue to try and get answers.

"What the fuck, Keith?"

"Sorry, Detective Stone, I didn't see you." Keith quickly apologized as he tried to keep the cookie from falling.

"What do you have there?" Stone asked with a confused look on his face. "Is that cookies?"

"Yes. I was on my way over to bring you some before they were all gone," Keith replied as he placed the cookies back on the paper plate.

"Really, Keith? You have to be shitting me. Those fucking cookies are evidence, and you are passing them around to the office? You are why I sometimes don't keep one in the chamber," Stone said as he pets his gun.

Keith stood there with a blank look on his face. He looked at the plate of cookies and looked up at Stone. It was almost as if you could see him working it all out in his face.

"OH! The cookies!" he said loudly. "The captain's wife made these and brought them in for everyone. They were going fast, so I grabbed some up for you."

"Oh," Stone replied. "I'm going down to the morgue to maybe put another body on ice"

Keith slowly placed down the plate and started walking back to his work area.

"Where are you going?" Stone asked.

"Back to my desk," Keith nervously replied.

"No." Stone shook his head. "You're coming with me."

RUFUS MONTGOMERY JR.

An excited Keith quickly fell in behind the detective. Keith was a big fan of Stones and had spent some time reading up on the detective's old cases. You can say he was well versed on everything Stone.

Stone stood there looking at the eager young man, turned and walked to the elevator. "Don't forget the cookies," Stone said, sending the young man running back for the plate. The click of the elevator button brought lights to life. The wait made Stone that much more irritated. How in the hell is there nothing to go on? Is this the case that gets me, the case that the great Detective Stone is unable solve? He played that room over and over in his head trying to see if he missed something. Anything would be better than what he had. There were no signs of forced entry. It was as if the front door was left open for someone. The neighbors said they did not hear or see anything out of the ordinary. It was a normal quiet night in the neighborhood. In fact, they said it is a lot quieter than it was when the soon to be ex-husband was living there. Stone wasn't sure if the window being open on such a cold night, had anything to do with anything. Could it have been open before the killer got there, or was it his way into the room? May even had been his way out of the room. But that wouldn't make any sense. Why go all the way down to the kitchen to get some oatmeal cookies just to come back upstairs to climb out of a window? I will be ruling that out. The victim was tied up and naked, but there were no clothes to speak of. None ripped up anywhere or even neatly folded and placed to the side.

"This elevator is so slow." Keith said, trying to break the silence.

Stone looked over at him. "Yes, it is slow as shit."

A loud ding went off just as he said that. "Look, Keith. There it is."

The door creaked and whined as it opened. A soft voice came from inside the elevator.

"Old building, old elevator."

They waited patiently to see who was in there talking. Her red hair, now down and no longer the victim of a paper hat, flowed down to the middle of Ronda's back. She stood there holding some folders and evidence bags. The doors finally fully opened, and the elevator shook to a stop.

"Wow. Guess I'm lucky to have made it this far in this thing," she said. "Are you two coming with?"

RUFUS MONTGOMERY JR.

They both nodded and stepped on. Stone turned around to face the doors. He looked down and saw his button was already pressed and glowing.

"What floor, boys?" Ronda asked.

"The same floor you're going to it seems. Headed to the morgue, are you?" Stone enquired.

"Yes. I am actually going to look at your body. Something about all that kept me up last night."

"Well, I hope you didn't keep Mr. Paper Hat up thinking about my case," Stone replied.

She smiled. "Did you see how he did that young man? He didn't miss a beat." She looked over at Keith to find him facing the back of the elevator. "What the fuck, Stone?"

"Yes, ma'am, he is a smooth one," Keith replied, never turning around.

Just then, the door opened in its normal elegant way. Ronda shook her head and stepped off. "Why the hell is he holding a plate of cookies? That's just weird."

Stone stood there, looking at Keith facing the back of the elevator. "Will you please turn around? Come the fuck on, will you?" Stone started down the hall after her.

Dark Whisper: The Fire That Burns Within

The long hall was not welcoming at all. The white tiled walls made you think how easy it would be to wash blood off them. The echo that every step made gave you the urge to look behind you. However, you dare not, in fear that the one time you do look back, there will be someone there. As for the smell, there was none. That entire floor smelled like nothing, good or bad. You would assume the floor of the building where dead bodies are stored would have a smell of some kind. Even when there is a body on the slab, the only smell that is noticeable is whatever perfume or aftershave the body had on it at the time of death. They stood there staring at her naked body. The color of her skin was no longer honey brown, and her lips were no longer a soft pink. The toenail polish she had on was still a maroon color. Her vagina was shaved within an inch of its life. She was expecting company. She had a faint white film on the inside of her thigh and on her vagina.

Stone pointed. "Is that evidence of rape?" He reached for a cookie. A look came over Stones face as he looked around the room. "Did the chef's wife happen to send any almond milk with the cookies?"

Ronda took a long look at him, then started to explain. "What you are seeing is not from him. What you are looking at is the dried remains of what happens to some women when they reach climax."

"You mean that is from her."

"Yes, Keith," Stone quickly interrupted.

"Anyway, boys, the slight bruising on her nose shows that it was probably held shut by something. Most likely by the fingers of whoever killed her."

"She wasn't sexually assaulted?" Stone asked, making certain he was getting this all right.

"Well, we are still trying to determine if it was assault, or some freaky shit gone wrong. I mean, there was a lot going on down there, and she was into it." Ronda walked to the foot of the table. "Look here." She pointed to the victim's toes. "What do you see?

"They're well-kept," Keith replied.

"Yes, but look how they're still loose and I can move them without problem. That tells me she was very much relaxed from the waist down. Then there are her hands ... those we had to pry open just to remove the silk scarves from them. That shows she was pulling on them when she was dying. The question is was it pain or pleasure that caused that?"

Stone and Ronda stood there looking at Keith. Stone sighed, reached over, and put Keith's hands back to his side. "No need to put your hands out. If you have a question, go ahead, ask. Okay, buddy?"

Keith nodded. "When you say pain or pleasure, what are you saying?"

"You take this one," Stone said as he grabbed the plate from Keith and sat in a chair nearby.

"Where do I start?" Ronda asked as she ran her fingers through her almost cartoony, but natural red hair.

"Let's say you're in pain and tied up. You are going to pull on your restraints desperately to stop whatever is causing the pain. It sounds horrible, I'm sure, but what we have found is that when a woman has been tied up during whatever sex game she may be partaking in, she tends to leave the same marks. During her orgasm or orgasms, she will pull on her restraints the same way."

"How exactly did you check that theory?" Stone asked with a mouth full of cookies.

"Really, Stone?" Ronda covered the body. "I am not entirely sure this was murder and not some sex game that got out of control and she ended up dead as a result of it."

Stone stood up with an irritated look on his face. "I take it you don't keep milk down here. I would think with all these freezers there would be milk in one."

Ronda shook her head as she walked over to Stone. "What are you doing about dinner tonight?"

"I don't have anything planned," Keith chimed in.

"You have work to do, Keith." Stone choked down the dry cookies. "I don't think I have anything going on. Why do you ask?"

"Because you and I can pick up something to eat on our way to the crime scene. I think we may have missed something, so I want to go over it again." Ronda helped herself to his last cookie.

"I think that would be a great idea. Just let me know what time works for you," Stone quickly replied.

"Good, good, then it's a date," she said, chewing on a piece of cookie, "but no need to dress up, we'll be wearing paper hats by the end of the night anyway."

Keith stood there watching Stone stare at Ronda's ass while she walked away. "Hey, Detective Stone, come on, I'll find you that milk." Keith made as much noise as he could with the door. As they walked down the creepy hallway, Keith turned to Stone. "Should I clear my evening as well?"

Why would you need to clear your evening, Keith?"

"Well, if we're going back to the scene, I'm going to need to make myself available, aren't I?"

"No, no, Keith. You absolutely do not need to make yourself available." The loud click of Stone pressing elevator button bounced off the walls. "I think we will be fine without you this time. Feel free to make plans for the evening—the entire evening.

"Ok?" Stone smiled as he stepped onto the elevator.

Back at his desk, Stone was going over the pictures of the inside of the house trying to familiarize himself before going back in. There had to be something he was missing. How is it that the perp walked in and out of there and left no trace behind? Not a print, not a hair—not even a footprint on the carpet. How much time did he have to get rid of both his and her DNA from the room? However, why clean up her DNA?

Why make it look like she was never in the room her body was actually found in? Who were the cookies for? None of it added up.

"Any luck on the cookie case, Stone?" A deep voice filled the room.

"No, captain." Stone shook his head. "No break in the case yet."

"Did you get some of the cookies my wife made? They were oatmeal raisin. Wait." The captain paused for a moment. "You didn't think it was the ones from your case, did you? I see how that could have happened."

Just then, Stone realized that he did it on purpose. "What kind of dick has his wife bake cookies just to fuck with me? You're a real dick Jim, a real fucking dick."

"What are you talking about? It was your grandmother's recipe, and it was not my idea. When I told your cousin about your case I woke up to laughter and the smell of cookies. I told her that one day she's going to get me shot, but she made me bring them anyway."

"Grandma's recipe?" Stone said. "No wonder they were so good." He reached for his glass of almond milk.

"That's almond milk, right, Stone?" Jim asked.

"What the fuck, Jim. You too?"

"You know, Stone, if it comes to pissing you off or her, you lose every time."

"I'm the one she used to beat up as a kid, so I get it, trust me."

"No hard feelings, detective?"

"Fuck you, captain."

"Good. Everyone back to work." Jim said as he closed his office door behind him.

The settling of the elevator echoed through the room. Bing! The elevator announced its arrival followed with the struggle of the doors opening. Its age showed. Ronda stepped off with her coat slung over her shoulder. Her hair was pulled back in a messy ponytail. The keys in hand jingled as she walked to the door. Upon entering, the room hung on the smell of her perfume and her every move. She found Stone staring at pictures of the scene.

"Detective Stone!" she shouted.

"What?" he replied, not looking up to even see who was calling his name.

RUFUS MONTGOMERY JR.

Keith cleared his throat a tapped Stone on his shoulder. "Look," he whispered.

Stone looked up to find Ronda staring at him from the door. A nervous smile found its way onto his face. With a soft, submissive voice, he answered, "Yes, Ronda, how can I help you?"

She held the door open. "Are you coming?" she motioned her head out.

"Oh, but of course. I was just taking a last look before our fieldtrip." He put everything away, grabbed his jacket, and walked to the door. Feeling a hand on his shoulder, Stone looked to see who it was.

"You sure you don't want me to come with?" Keith asked, making sure his presence would not be needed. Stone took a long look at him before he spoke. "Keith, get the hell away from me, you weirdo." As Stone got to the door and held it open for Ronda, she shouted back at Keith, "Don't be late tomorrow! We still have a lot of work to do, buddy!"

10

"YOU HAVEN'T SAID MUCH AT ALL ON THE way here. What's that about?" Ronda asked as she put the menu down and picked up her milkshake. She raised an eyebrow.

"I was pretty sure I was going to be the next one dead and naked on a slab. I almost got out and kissed the ground when you parked the car. For an officer of the law, you have little regard for the laws of the road," Stone said.

Ronda held some of the milkshake in her mouth, savoring the taste. "This place has the best chocolate shakes in town." She took another small sip. "I take it you don't approve of my driving skills?" An innocent look crossed her face. "As far as you naked on a slab, the night is still young."

Stone looked blankly at Ronda and took a drink of his coffee. "Why did you say you weren't sure her dying was intentional? Then you said that she was a willing participant of whatever it was that took place. All because of her toes being relaxed."

Ronda put her straw to Stone's lips. "You have to try this shake, it's amazing."

Stone sat there.

"Fine, take a sip and I'll tell you," she said as she tapped his lips with the straw.

He shook his head, leaned forward, and took a sip. She could see his eyes light up. She smiled at him.

"See, I told you it was the best in town." She slowly pulled the straw back a bit. "Now, for your question. A deal is a deal. Well," she said, "when I was in college studying crime scene investigation, we came across a case similar to this one, where the woman was tied up the same way. Just like this one, I thought it was sex games gone wrong. The professor insisted that I was wrong. Years after I got married, my husband and I were into some ... let's say ... strange things."

"What do you mean strange things?" Stone asked as he helped himself to another sip of the chocolate shake.

"Well, we re-enacted the scene from that case. It left the same marks, and everything from my waist down was like spaghetti noodles. This case takes me back to all of that."

"If it was an accident, why not call the police and explain that? Why stop for cookies before leaving? If what you're saying is true, he was scared and knew to wipe the room clean. Him stopping for a snack on his way out ... that is not a thing. That is what I'm finding hard to understand."

"Here's the thing, if we spend too much time trying to make sense of why people do the madness they do, we're going to miss the meathead behind it all, and that's how they get away with it." Ronda ordered him is own milkshake.

"Thank you. They are as good as you said they were."

"Don't thank me, I just gave you a taste. I didn't think I would be sharing it." Ronda laughed.

Stone turned her left hand over. "Do you not wear the ring to work? You said you were married."

"Yes," Ronda replied, "I was married, but not anymore."

"What happened? If you don't mind me asking?"

Ronda smiled. "Remember me saying that we were into strange things?"

RUFUS MONTGOMERY JR.

Stone shook his head up and down.

"Well, he forgot the safe word and things got real for him." She smiled. "He said he no longer felt safe around me, and rightly so. Things got crazy for him but fucking fun for me." She let out an ominous laugh. "Look." She pointed. "Your shake is here."

Stone slowly picked up his frozen milky beverage, keeping his eyes fixed on Ronda the entire time. He didn't know if he should've been excited or afraid of what she just told him. Here he was, sitting across from a smart, strong, and beautiful woman that also seemed to have a healthy sex drive. The best part was that she seemed to be into some real freaky shit. "Worth it?"

"What was that?" Ronda asked, not sure what Stone meant.

"Nothing," he replied as he licked the shake from his lips. "I was just thinking out loud. This milkshake was so worth coming to this place. Thanks for introducing me to it." He smiled at Ronda.

Their food finally came to the table, and not a moment too soon. Ronda cut her burger in half to see if her steak was red enough in the middle. A thin drip of blood ran down the side of it, leaving a pink trail behind. She picked up one of her curly fries, leaned her head back and slowly lowered it into her mouth. Stone watched as she swallowed it whole. At that moment, his mind wandered. What he saw was a little different to what was really taking place. There Ronda sat on the edge of the bed looking up at him wearing nothing but dark purple panties. Her red hair draped over her breasts only hiding her left nipple. As she stared at him, those green, glowing eyes looking through his very soul. She began to run her hand down his naked chest, then folded her fingers into his pants, pulling him closer. Unbuckling his belt, she leaned in to kiss his stomach with just the right amount of tongue. As she pulled his pants down, he stepped out of them with his hard cock inches from her face. She gently kissed the shaft while looking up at him. She pushed him back a little as he started to lower his dick into her warm, wet…

"Stone! I'm talking to you about your fucking case and you're over there daydreaming?" She scolded him. "You have to be fucking shitting me."

Stone smiled. "I shit you not." They both laughed. "What were you saying again?" he asked as he shoved one of his fries into his mouth.

"Now that I have your attention, let's start over. From what Larry and the rest of the team could tell, whoever it was did not break into the house, but they did not come through the front door either. They did find that the alarm was not armed either. Most likely, she was expecting the killer. Otherwise, why would she have left it turned off? She was a newly single woman living on her own."

"Do you always arm your alarm? Don't you ever forget to arm it?" Stone asked, trying to play devil's advocate, and making sure every possibility was considered.

Ronda stopped to think. "I have not turned it on right away when I first get in, on occasion. Maybe I get distracted or have my arms full and only have in mind and rush to disarm it before the alarm starts going off. After that, I start putting things away, take my shoes off, and maybe start dinner. I may even pour myself a drink, or someone calls. So, there are many reasons and ways she could have left it off unintentionally."

"Would you say baking could be distracting enough to throw you off your routine?" Stone asked. "Her soon to be ex-husband did say she hated raisins. Wouldn't you say baking a recipe that uses raisins to be somewhat of a change from the norm for her? I still can't wrap my head around the cookie thing."

"That's another reason she knew who killed her. They did not have conventional sex, but she did orgasm, from what we could tell. We haven't told anyone else about this, but her DNA was found somewhere else, even though there was no trace of her in her room."

Stone leaned forward with his eyes fixed on Ronda's lips, hanging on her every word. "What did your forensic team find?"

"I asked Larry to have one of his guys swab the cookie trays for DNA, and dust for prints. There were no prints found, but we did find vaginal secretion where some of the cookies were missing. He left some of her DNA on the tray. That proves that at some point, he had his hand inside her or on her wet vagina. Other than that, there is not much else to go on." Ronda's teeth cut through the meat. "Did you have Keith look into any similar open cases in Seattle?"

RUFUS MONTGOMERY JR.

"You mean cases where people were found dead, and cookies were missing? I wouldn't know where to start that search. As strange as this case is, I will have him look into any unsolved cases that stand out from the others. How old was she again?" Stone reached for his phone.

Ronda flipped through some of the papers spread on the table. "It says here that she is thirty-eight, no kids, and going through a divorce. Have you ever been married, Stone?"

Stone tried to hide his struggle to breathe after a gulp of milkshake. His shoulders tensed up. He gathered himself. "I got real close one time, but it wasn't meant for me. Who knows, I may take another shot at it one day, but for now, I think I'll just keep putting bad guys away."

"I always found that statement interesting." Ronda tilted her head, showing her disapproval.

"What statement is that, young lady?" Stone inquired.

"The saying "Bad Guys." Who are these bad guys, and can't any one of us be one? Is the term only for those who have done terrible things, or does it also apply to those who have not yet had the opportunity to do the bad or evil acts we are all capable of? Just a year ago, how many of these perps did

Internal Affairs pick up from the same station we work? They were some of the good guys until they were not. Just something to think about."

The thought of good and evil being so simple didn't add up to her. Her own thoughts scared her sometimes. The decision not to do what those voices whispered was simply the only thing keeping her from being one of the bad people they hunted. She thought back to the genuine fear on her ex-husbands face when she did not stop after the safe word. Him forgetting the word or being in discomfort and being unable to say it meant all bets were off. Yes, she could have stopped, but why? The power that she held at that moment filled her with so much pleasure. She could have stopped but didn't want to.

"You're saying that any of us are capable of what this guy did to this woman?" Stone asked, still trying to digest what Ronda said.

"Yes, very much so. Tell me, have you ever had thoughts that most people would see as evil or downright wrong? What stopped you from acting on them? Maybe you would've been better off if you did act upon it. Ask yourself if you're the man who chooses not to listen to those voices. Or are you ignoring the real you in those voices that whisper?"

"What you're saying is that the question we should ask is deeper than just being good or bad people?" Stone asked, trying to make sense of Ronda's statement. "Are we the people we let the world see, or are we what we tuck away and hide from the world?"

"It seems like you get it, detective." Ronda leaned back and lowered another fry into her mouth. "We can think like them and that's the best way to catch these so-called bad guys we hunt. Let's say her dying was not a mistake during a sex game and his intention was coming there to kill her. Did he bring a weapon? Why does it seem like he was let in, and why were snacks left for him? Since there wasn't conventional sex, are we entirely sure it was a man and not a woman?"

"I would still say a man just from how big his hands would have to be to cover both her nose and mouth. That or we are looking for a very large woman. In fact, let me see your hands, Ronda?"

Ronda put both hands up showing only one finger on each. "Aren't these the fingers that were used? They are two of my favorites, for sure. Could my hands be big enough to be the hands of the killer?"

"We are not entirely sure those were the fingers that were used, but those meaty stubs of yours could very well be the ones in question." Stone held her hands and examined them. "Maybe we should put these into evidence. Do me a favor and don't leave town. I may have questions for you."

"Yes, Detective Stone. I will do my best to stay close. Make sure not to forget the safe word when it starts to hurt too much." Ronda slowly pulled her hands free.

The server coughed loudly, reminding the two that they were not alone. "Can I get you anything else?"

"No, I think we are good," Stone said, making the universal sign with his hand for the check.

"No dessert this evening?"

"Maybe, but I have to see if he deserves anything sweet later." Ronda replied, keeping her eyes fixed on Stone the entire time. The sound of the remainder of milkshake making its way up the straw broke the silence. Stone put down the empty cup and licked what was left off of his mouth. "This should cover it." Stone stood up and put his wallet away. He held the door open and said, "I'm driving."

"What?" Ronda asked as she dropped her keys into his palm. "I'm concluding you're not a fan of my driving. I got us here safe enough, didn't I?"

"No, timing and my grandmother praying for me every Saturday got me here alive."

Ronda stood in the doorway and looked at Stone. "If you didn't feel safe then you should have used the safe word." She pointed to the door. Stone hit the key fob and unlocked door. The chirp rang out and she climbed into the car.

RONDA SAT ON THE EDGE OF THE OPEN TRUNK. Pulling off the modest heels she had on, she wiggled her toes and rubbed them. Normally, she would wear more comfortable shoes, but they wouldn't have propped her ass up just right to keep Stone's eyes on her. She handed a pair of paper shoes to the detective. He smiled and put them in his pocket, reached down, and picked up her shoes and placed them in the trunk. The slam cut through the silence of the quiet neighborhood. Ronda rubbed her bare feet on the CSI blanket that was placed at the front door. She put on the first pair, almost losing her balance in the process. Stone took the paper shoes left in her hand and opened it for her. Holding onto the back of his neck, she slid her other foot in.

"God this bitch loves potpourri," she said as she covered her nose. "It wasn't this strong before, was it?" Ronda fanned her hands in front of her face.

"I think with all the running around, and with the doors open, I guess I didn't take notice. You are right, though. This is a bit much," Stone said.

"I think maybe I get what his motives were, and I can't say I blame him." Ronda walked up the stairs, her gloved hand sticking to the banister.

They trudged through the house trying to climb into the mind of this killer. They had to make sense of why he or she killed that night. Upon entering the room where the body was found, a more pleasant smell filled their noses.

"Now, this smell I do remember," Stone said, taking a deep breath. "Whatever it was that she had on that night was intoxicating. Was your team able to find out the name of what lotion she was wearing that night?"

"We were testing all her lotions, then had it narrowed down to one." Ronda walked over to the closed window. "We found a partial print on the dresser."

"He missed something?" Stone asked.

"No," she replied. "He or she didn't miss anything. He left that print to fuck with us."

Intrigued, Stone walked over to the window. "Fucking with us? How can leaving a print fuck with us? Either it's her print, meaning he didn't fully erase her from the room, or even better, he left his partial print when he was cleaning up."

Ronda shook her head. "No."

"No to which one?" Stone threw his shoulders up.

"The print was made, not left. When a print is left, it is on the surface of whatever it's left on."

"Yes, I get that," Stone replied

"Well, the print that we found was meticulously carved into the lotion bottle that she used that night. We are still running it to see if anything comes back, but none of us are very hopeful."

"You're telling me this son of a bitch took the time to carve fingerprints into a bottle of lotion before stopping for a snack on his way out? Who the fuck are we dealing with here?"

Ronda put her hand on her waist. "That's what we're doing here." Looking up at him, her green eyes reflected the moonlight. "We're trying to get into the mind of this killer with a taste for cookies. Speaking of that, maybe we would have more luck in the kitchen. Come with me." She walked around him running her left hand from his right hip across the front of him tracing the lower edge of his belt all the way around to his left hip. His gun shifted slightly from his pants losing space inside of them. The smell of her hair gave the same effect of a third shot of tequila. Intoxicating. Stone followed her down to the kitchen. He watched as her skirt ran up the back of her thighs as she examined the lower part of the refrigerator for the second time. He made sure to keep the island between the two of them.

"What are you expecting to find in there?" Stone asked, trying to get a better look in the refrigerator.

RUFUS MONTGOMERY JR.

"What was it that you were trying so hard to get your hands on back at the morgue?" Ronda said, sliding bottles around.

Stone folded his top lip. "Another cookie? After you stole my last one."

Ronda looked back at him. "No, you ass. Milk. You wanted milk to wash down the cookies. I was thinking maybe he wanted something to wash down his snack as well, but there's no sign of him in this house. Get over here and help me look, will you?" Ronda slid the bottom drawer closed.

Adjusting his gun, Stone slowly walked around the island. He started going through the top of the fridge, hoping she wouldn't notice the bulge in his pants.

"And, again, nothing." Ronda stood up. "Timing is everything."

"What do you mean?" Stone asked, stepping back, wondering if she felt it as she grazed against his crotch.

"Too late to back up now. I already know it's there. Since there's no one else here, it's for me, and I see no reason why I shouldn't have it." Ronda stepped back into it. "Yep, I was right. That there is a hard dick, is it not, detective?" She turned to face him. Her hands gripped his belt. Using it as leverage, she bit his bottom lip, and then pushed past him towards the island. Putting her hands on either side of it, she leaned ever so slightly forward patiently waiting. Her body trembled from the surprise of his cold hands rub her thighs. He took in the smell of her hair as he gripped the bottom of her skirt, peeling it up over her just enough to see where her underwear started to gather between her checks. Not purple, as he had imagined, but green and just as sexy. She leaned forward and pushed her ass back. Her knees hit the island as he slowly ran his hands down her legs. With his knees behind her, he grabbed the front of her thighs and pulled her legs apart. His finger caressed between her underwear and her wet vagina. Moving them out of the way, he replaced them with his tongue, first softly tapping her clit with it. You could hear the slipping of her gloves as her grip tightened. Her lips pulsated on his tongue letting him know he had it right where she wanted it. Stone didn't stop until he had his fill and she let him know she wanted more of him inside her. He got back to his feet, and wiped his chin, leaving his gloved finger in her. To her, the sound of his zipper took what seemed like forever. After feeling his right hand on her back, she felt him slowly slide into her. Her back arched as she pushed herself the rest of the way onto him. The two of them moved gently together. He'd pull back a little, and she'd meet him halfway, pulling away just enough to make him work for some of it. Stone gripped her hips tighter and became more aggressive. Ronda could feel him growing inside her as her groans got more intense.

"Do you want me to pull out?" Stone asked between thrusts.

"No!" She moaned. "Leave it in. Come inside me." She reached around pulling him deeper in. "I want to feel it." Her body started to shake then tense up as she stopped moving. Stone growled as the warmth of his cum filled her. The napkin holder on the counter broke as Ronda gripped it. She passed it back to Stone. "We shouldn't leave any of our DNA behind either."

They both laughed.

She got one of the paper towels and cleaned herself.

"Guess there's nothing else here for us to find, Ronda."

"No, I would say not, detective. This guy is good. We're going to have to get lucky." Ronda said, stopping outside the doorway and taking off the paper shoes.

"Was not pulling out the best idea?" Stone asked, holding her waist.

"I don't see why not." She bounced up to kiss him. "You're my boyfriend now." She walked barefoot down the driveway. Once again leaving Stone with his thoughts.

RUFUS MONTGOMERY JR.

11

AS I STEPPED OFF THE LIFT, I HEARD CHAOS in the normally quiet lobby. That is music to my ears. Someone is causing a ruckus. Looks like someone has misplaced their wallet. It could not have happened to a nicer person. I could not hide the joy of it in my face. I smile the smile of a guilty boy who took that cookie when mother was not looking. I can tell that the front desk manager doesn't give a shit about him or his wallet. Yet he's still giving the man all the attention he wants all while just wanting him to go away. His credit card is already on file, and the room is already paid for. It was just a billfold with only cash in it. If he keeps this behavior up, I may just have to put him on my list of things to do while in the UK. I should see if there's anything I can do to help.

"Excuse me?" I approach the center of the chaos. "I could not help but to overhear what was going on." I'm calm and polite with my tone. Then I say what sets all rich assholes off. Get ready for this one. "If you're a little short, I can help cover whatever it is that you need." Now the fun begins. This man may just kill himself. He turns and looks over at me. If looks could kill, my black ass would have just become the victim. I keep a shit-eating grin on my face. You know the one. Stacy has threatened several times to slap this same grin off my moisturized face.

He balls up his hand that once rested on the front desk. The only thing I can think is how great of a story this is going to be. His eyes glaze over as he places his left hand on the center of my chest and pushes me. "Get the FUCK away from me, you bloody CUNT! I have FUCKING money!" His voice echoes through the lobby. It takes everything in me not to die laughing. This is going better than I planned. This man is really fucking upset. I should just walk away at this point, but of course I won't. "It's ok," I say as I reach for my wallet. "I'm sure you're good for it."

"I don't need your money, you little shit!" He storms to me.

RUFUS MONTGOMERY JR.

"Now, now." The hotel manager tries to take his attention away from me. "We will do our best to find the wallet you misplaced."

An employee walks by with a clear garbage bag filled with trash. The napkin must have come off because there is his wallet pressed against the bag. I can no longer hold back my laughter.

"Hey, friend," I say. "Is that the wallet all this fuss is about?" I stop the employee and take the bag from him to get a closer look. "You are right. You do have money. That's a nice-looking wallet. It looks very expensive. Well, here you go. Problem solved," I say as I hand him the bag.

"I'm not getting it out of there," he says.

I smile as I step in close. "Yes, you are." I look down at my chest. "Don't forget, I owe you one."

We all look on as he fishes his wallet out of the trash.

"You're going to want to clean that off before you use that again, my friend," I add as I continue to the exit.

The blanket of night drapes over London. The sweet air kisses my face when I open the lobby doors. "Night," I whisper to myself. God, I love the night and the feel of it all. It brings out something in the people who are willing to come out and move around in the darkness—those who use it as a cover and a way to hide their doings under the night's blanket. Walking out into the brisk damp air, I close my eyes and take in a deep breath. Now, to find this pub Vicky told me about. I'm not working tonight, so I can use the GPS on my phone. It should be easy enough to find, I hope. I have to ask why so many of the pubs in London have an Irish name. What the fuck is that all about? Or there is some kind of drunken animal in the name. Anyway, let's see who and what is out tonight.

    I'm wearing nothing fancy, just jeans and a long sleeve shirt paired with gray Converse and a blazer. It's my look. I hope she likes it. It is about a fifteen, twenty-minute walk from my hotel, close to where I rescued her from the puddle. As I approach the Flying Monkey, it seems to be a pretty happening place. There's a good crowd of people, and I see some dancing going on. I fucking love the British. I walk in and a drunk English man throws his arm over my shoulders and pulls me over to a bar with him and the rest of his mates. "Seven shots for me and my mates!" he shouts to the bar keep. Seven shots of what the fuck ever is poured, and we drink. We shout, hug, and order another round of shots. You got to love this city and its people. As I'm downing my second or fifth shot, off to the corner at a table alone is Vicky looking at me with a smile on her face. Her beautiful teardrop-shaped face is a welcoming sight.

"I got the next round! Eight shots this time!" I shout to the bar keep. "You guys are going to make me late for my date." I laugh and overpay the bar keep, covering their next couple of rounds. I grab two of the drinks, bid my new friends good drinking, and walk over to Vicky and our table for two.

"Who's that second shot for?" she asks as I place them down.

"Second shot?" I reply. "They're both for you, my dear. First one is for you not coming over there to save me from the local rugby team."

She laughs. "The second shot is for what?"

"Second drink is you needing to catch up, young lady." I take her cup of water and drink almost half of it. She smiles, shakes her head, and starts to take the first shot. Her curly dirty blond hair bounces as she starts in on the first shot. Her full lips leave a sweet pink memory of her on the glass. She throws her head back with the second shot, as everything slows down. I take a long look at her smooth, full neck as she swallows. Her lips press on the glass, and her hair drapes her shoulders. Everything in the pub goes quiet. The sound of the shot glass hitting the table brings it all back.

"You happy now?" She smiles and slides one of the glasses across the table at me. "See, all gone." She turns the other glass over.

She has my attention as I lean forward and lick my bottom lip—a bad habit of mine when I am guessing how someone tastes. She sits across from me, her shoulders covered with a light cardigan over her sleeveless top. I can tell she put a little more work into how she looks tonight. She's wearing a bit more makeup, and her hair is done in a sexy "Yes I like you, but I do not want you thinking I did too much" kind of way. Since she's sitting, the table hides if she is wearing pants, a skirt, or a dress. Though it does not even matter. Her awkward personality is so captivating because of the confidence she has. She is a woman that's comfortable in her skin, no matter what that skin looks like. I find that extremely attractive and appealing. It will be interesting to see how she takes me if I stop playing human for a little and just be myself. Nope, do not think she's the type to get her hands bloody.

"Vicky, tell me about yourself." I pull my chair in closer.

She purses her lips before replying, "What would you like to know, Jason?"

What you taste like is the first thing that comes to mind. "What do you do for a living?"

"Well, I work for the UK government, in a way." I can tell she's trying not to reveal too much, but that makes me that much more intrigued.

"Is that right?" I rewind to this morning when we first met. I remember her shoes were very conservative, black skirt, light blue top. The paperwork she handed me to hold were in a manila folder with names written on the tabs. I can recall one saying, "Not Cleared for Duty." I will have to check to see what government buildings are in walking distance from where we were this morning.

"Yes," she replies as she reaches for her cup of water. She takes a drink—a clear sign of trying to change the conversation from a subject she does not want to talk about. "Let's just say I spend my day inside of other people's heads and leave it at that for now." She tilts her head to the right and raises her eyebrows.

"What do you do?" she asks, redirecting. I saw that coming.

"I work for an artist. I travel around setting up gallery showings and sales of his paintings. Nothing too exciting." The more information I give leaves less room for unwanted questions. It's a little trick.

"Wow, I love art. Do you do any drawing of your own?"

"I try my hand at art here and there, but nothing I think anyone would want to spend their hard-earned money on."

"Boy, I wish I could draw or paint myself." The look of excitement on her face is great. "My sister would always make fun of me when I tried my hand at art. She would always tell me that cave paintings belonged in caves and not on the ice box."

"That's not right. I'm sure they weren't that bad. Your mum liked them, so there is that."

"Oh, thanks." She kicks me. "That's like telling a girl at least your mum thinks you're pretty."

"If I said that I would be lying, because I think you're beautiful." I let the words escape my mouth before my brain has time to process them. Now I have done it. Her face is turning a shade of pink. I need to bring her back to the conversation. "So, you have a sister? Any other siblings?" I put her back on comfortable footing.

"I have an older and a younger brother. I'm a middle child, so I could sometimes go unseen by others. You spotting me in this crowded pub, and now looking at me for as long as you have is something I am not use to at all. I keep wondering if there is something on my face that you can't stop looking at." She pulls a mirror from her purse to check for just that.

I reach across and grab the mirror and her hand. "Put it away. It's you and only you that I'm looking at. I spend my days around art, so I know when I see something I like to look at. Therefore, you will actually catch me staring at you." By the look on her face, she's just unknowingly stepped into my world. Most women have a preconceived idea of what beauty is and spend their time pointing out their flaws.

"How do you do it?" she asks

Confused as to what she means, I ask, "How do I do what?"

Dark Whisper: The Fire That Burns Within

She smiles. I can see her cheeks fill with blood. She takes a deep breath. "How do you pick paintings to be shown in galleries if your eyes are that bad that you think me beautiful. That has to be a problem for you in your line of work."

"Do you not think I know what beauty is because I find you beautiful? Sounds to me like you are the one that's not clear on what beauty is. Would you like to know why you aren't hard to look at?"

"Jason," she says, "I would love to know why you are staring at me. It's kind of creepy."

"Well," I say, "a beauty that you can't quite put your finger on is a true beauty—a real definition of beauty. When you don't know exactly why it's beautiful, but you know you would happily give a year off your life just for one more glimpse of her face, and her smile." I lean over the table. "That piece of hair that falls perfectly out of place—all of that is what love stories are made of. Real love stories. Not the ones in fiction books. Love stories aren't perfect, because if they were, they would be boring."

RUFUS MONTGOMERY JR.

Resting her chin on her two balled up fists, she asks, "Really boring. How would a not boring, not perfect love story start if you were writing this book?"

"Well, I am in no way a writer, but if I were to write a love story, it would start with an extremely handsome man rescuing an awkward girl's feet from a cold puddle of water."

"Hey! Who you bloody calling awkward? I had everything under control. You just have a thing with me. I wouldn't be surprised if you're a serial killer with a foot fetish here in London only to look for British feet to take back from holiday as some kind of trophy."

I laugh. "You have some kind of imagination. Maybe you're the writer and should be telling me how you would write the perfect tale of love." I call the waiter over and order us two soft drinks and two more shots. She looks at me as to say, "Really?" but she does not stop me.

"My story would start with the girl not being awkward, and the guy not as handsome," she says, and then sticks her tongue out at me.

I laugh and wonder if I really like her. I only ask myself that because I have not thought of killing her once tonight. That can't be right. Something must be up. "Let's make her awkwardly beautiful, and him socially awkward and terrible with women. Is that a better start for your love story?" I could look at her smile all night. The truth of who she is lives in her face. She is everything I am not. "Do you like what you do for a living? I mean, I think it's very important that people like what they spend most of their time doing."

"We're spending a lot of time speaking about me. I would like to know more about my savior from that deadly puddle. Tell me more about you." She manages to bring up my most hated subject. Where do I start? I am a functioning sociopath that paints million-dollar paintings that I take no credit for. I was planning to kill my assistant, but instead I spent this afternoon with her pussy in my mouth in the back of a limo. What else is there, let me think ...oh! I sexually harassed a girl at lunch today. And there is this man in my hotel that I am pretty certain I am going to kill before I leave London, because he's a dick.

"Tell me about your family. Do you have siblings?" Her voice steps in my head, interrupting my train of thought.

RUFUS MONTGOMERY JR.

"We could start there," I say, thinking aloud. "I come from a big family. I'm the first of eight."

"Wow," she replies. "That is a big family. That's must have been great." She doesn't know how wrong she is.

"Great is not exactly the word I would use to describe things." I take a sip of my drink.

"Why is that?" she asks, a sad look on her face. "Aren't you close with them?"

"Oh, we're good. We try our best to stay in touch and keep a strong relationship with one another. Life sometimes gets in the way, but we do our best." I quickly clear that up for her.

"What about your parents?" Her follow up question comes strong and on point. I try to hide my asshole grin.

"I was born to the greatest woman I know." I take my shot and signal for another.

"You and your mother are close?" she asks.

"No," I quickly reply. "My grandmother. I was born to her, not them." I lick my lips, now dry from the thought of the question I know is coming next.

Her eyes narrow. She is now interested in my answer to her next question. "Are you close with your father?"

There it is. She has opened up my coffin and is now asking for death to show his face.

"Let me paint you a picture," I say, trying to take back some control. "As the first of eight kids, I quickly realized I was just practice. Don't get me wrong, I was fed, clothed, and given a roof. I had all that a human child would need to survive and not much else. As for the inner workings of what a person should be, well, that part I was on my own to figure out myself. Any bit of humanity I managed to pick up was what my grandmother gave me in the form of unconditional love."

She has the saddest look on her face as I speak. "The million-dollar question is did they ever have a plan for me? Some kind of thought of what they wanted me to be, or any expectations. That is fine as well. My plan worked out nonetheless."

It's as if she really heard everything, I just said without actually saying it. She's summed it all up.

"What you are saying is that your grandmother is what is tethering you to humanity with not the love she has for you, but because of the love you have for her?"

I smile and think to myself how the fuck.

"I'm going to get you one more drink, and then we are going for a walk. I want to spend some time with you out in the night air. Is that okay with you, Vicky?"

She closes her eyes, smiles, and shakes her head. "Yes, Jason. That would be nice."

We exchange a few more jokes before I take her over to my new friends. I order another round including one for Vicky. The pub roars "Bye Vicky!" when we exit the threshold. "Bye guys!" she shouts back as I put my arm around her hips and usher her out the door.

She places her hand on my chest, stops me under a streetlamp, and looks up at me. "You have a way with people," she says, trying to find my deep brown eyes as the streetlight flickers above us. "Is that normal for you?" she asks, placing her hand on my chin, maneuvering my face in a way that she could better see my eyes.

"Is what normal?" I ask, unaware of what she means.

She licks her lips. "Are people normally drawn to you like everyone in that pub was?" She clarified her question.

Unsure how to respond, I simply say, "Not everyone." I hope she drops the subject, but by how she's squished her face at me, I can tell it did not work. I am in for more questioning.

"Do you always use humor as a distraction when someone is trying to get to know you?"

"To know me?" I ask, feigning confusion.

"Yes, get to know you and not the Jason everyone excepts as the real you?" she says.

I want to answer her and tell her "No, I do not always use humor to avoid answering questions about myself, sometimes I just kill the person if they get too close to figuring me out. Oh, and I sometimes, I make it look like an accident." However, I answer a different way, as to not send her running down the street. "No, I only sometimes use humor." I gently place my hand around her waist and pull her closer into me. Her body is warm and all I can think of is how it would feel to have my hands covered in her blood. "You smell so good," I say as I leaned over and take her in.

She lets out the cutest little giggle. "You're not going to give me a straight answer, I see."

RUFUS MONTGOMERY JR.

"People find me interesting." I answer her question. "I'm a very closed off person and stay pretty much to myself. I think others somehow sense that and go out of their way to make it past my defenses and get to know me. Kind of what your sweet-smelling ass is trying to do right now."

"No," she replies. "When I first met you, all I wanted was for you to let go of my foot. That cute little thing you do is not getting you out of answering me. Out with a straight answer, creepy foot man."

"Who am I, you ask? I am truly that guy you've been warned about and told to stay far away from. I have been known to make women go absolutely mad. Some have tried to kill themselves, and some have tried to kill me. There have even been those who have tried to kill other women because I've shown interest in them. Simply put, I bring out the worst in some people if they stick around long enough. I don't lie to myself and say these women are crazy, because I truly know I'm the cause of their temporary madness. Please do not think their behavior is due to cruel treatment on my part. It is just the opposite. As you saw tonight, I treat others well, and those I care for I treat that much better. I will open doors and pull out your chair for you. Kiss you on that spot where your back ends and your ass begins. Turn you over and kiss just close enough to all the parts of you that you want me to put my mouth on the most. When I can feel your wetness, and taste you on my lips, I will start taking parts of you in my mouth."

I could not tell by how she was looking if I had answered her question or not.

"I think I'm bleeding," I say as I push my hand under the hair on the back of her head.

"What?" she asks, confused.

"Your nails in my side. I think you have broken the skin." As I speak, her grip on me increases to the point where I think she has opened me up a bit. By answering her question, she managed to show me a bit about herself. With her face and my shirt both turning red, she loosens her hold on me. "Is there anything else you would like to know about me, miss?"

Her wanting brown eyes gaze into me. It is an uncomfortable feeling. With her bottom lip between her teeth, she shakes her head no. I can feel the heat rising off her body.

"Does it hurt?" Vicky asks as she rubs me gently.

RUFUS MONTGOMERY JR.

"Only when you rub it like that," I reply. "You're just rubbing my shirt into it right now. I can't say it's a pleasant feeling." I think to myself how good the pain feels. It's hard to feel much of anything. Sometimes, pain is very much welcomed. Smiling awkwardly, Vicky places her hand on my chest, putting some space between the two of us. It is as if she doesn't want me to know she is wet. By how firmly her teeth holds her lip, she gave up her little secret.

"We better get going before my mates drag us back in for another round of drinks." I take her hands in mine, and bring them up, giving her what she wants. Placing my face in her hands, I gave her the upper hand, letting her know I was putting myself in her mercy. "Are you going to show me around your city?"

God, her smell is amazing. It is as if she's made of fruit. We walk around London, and she takes me to places I never would have seen. There's this one place we go that has the best falafels I have ever tasted. I can't help but to wonder if Vicky tastes as good. More on the fruitier side, I would imagine. We stand eating as we watch pissed British people in their natural habitat as she explains why that woman put hands on that man.

Dark Whisper: The Fire That Burns Within

Then she tells me why you should never call a woman a "Fat Cow," like that is something I would do anyway. I shake my head as the drunken man lets those words pass his lips. The shear force behind the slap confirms to me it was indeed not the thing to do.

We gingerly walk past the commotion. Best to be on our way. Her arm in mine helps me forget about the fact that I can see my breath when I exhale. I always find myself back in this city even when I'm not here for work. Even Stacy is unaware of how often I am here, or for how long I stay when I am in London. When I am here for an extended period, I stay in the tiny home I purchased in Preston. It feels a bit more like home than a hotel room in the city. It always amazes me how alive the city is even on a weekday. The clubs and pubs still fill with people celebrating something or the other, or just out with friends tying on a few trying to put another workday behind them.

I'm out tonight trying to decide what to do with this delightful little creature beside me. Can I look her in those beautiful eyes and watch the life leave them? That may be a challenge. The longer I keep her out, the more about me she will reveal. I should really take her home.

"Do you work in the morning?" I ask, trying to show my concern. "Wouldn't want you falling asleep at work. Furthermore, by the sound of things, your work requires you to have your wits about you. Would that be a correct assumption?" I pull her in closer. At this point, she has shown that she enjoys having her body close to mine. Moreover, it's sweet when she gently pats the holes she put in me earlier.

"You are correct in your assumption," she replies, patting me ever so gently. Pat, pat, pat. She presses her crotch against my leg. It is cold enough out to where I can see our breath becoming one in the space between us. Yet, the heat coming off her pussy on to my leg is almost overwhelming. If not her, someone will be paying for what her pussy is doing to me.

"Is this your way of bringing our evening to an end, Jason?" A playful smile creeps slowly onto Vicky's full pink lips. "Or have you had enough of my British humor? I find myself charming." She folds her bottom lip in.

Before I know it, I have her top lip between mine. Her lips taste as good as she smells. Is this woman made out of candy or something? She should taste more like onions with all they put in our falafels. Yet somehow, she still tastes so very sweet. The patting becomes a firm grip, and now, she has my bottom lip between her lips with her tongue advancing into my mouth. I run my hands down from her shoulder using my fingers to tracing the outline of her body. It is cold, but for the first time tonight her body starts to tremble. The closer my fingers get to the small of her back, the more aggressively her body shakes. If I keep this up, Vicky will very well pull my bottom lip free from my face. When I finally reach the spot where her back becomes the top of her ass, I pull her in tight. Her tongue stiffens in my mouth and her shaking ends. She is mine if I wish to have her.

When we are once again two people, we stand looking at each other, unable to bring ourselves to words. Am I playing human, or is she really seeing me? Not the made-up Jason Miller the world outside gets to see. Is she seeing me as the man my grandmother sees when she looks into the eyes of her son? Could she know me as the name my grandmother looked into my crib and called me? This is all too much and all too soon. I'm in London on business, not pleasure. Although, in a way, death is also my business and I do sometimes take pleasure in death. Is Vicky business or pleasure? My dick is screaming pleasure, but he has never been trustworthy. In fact, I remember taking away his voting rights. This guys a felon.

"I am in no way ready for this night to end," I say, breaking the silence. "But for the first, and probably the last time, I am going to play the adult and send you to bed." I hear myself say those words, and I hate myself for saying them. "If you will allow me, I would love to walk you home." If I remember correctly, we are close to where we met earlier today, so she must not live too far from here. Will she let the man her parents warned her about walk her life walk her home?

Still in my arms, Vicky reaches up and holds my face in her hands and pulls me down to her. Taking my bottom lip once again in her mouth, she gives it a gentle but firm suck. "I will take a taxi home," she says as she lowers herself down from my lips. She turns to hail a taxi. "Can't have you knowing where I live just yet." She smiles that playful smile, then adds, "Who knows, you could be a very charming serial killer that wants to fuck me then kill me. Although, right now, only half of that plan would be something I could really go for. If you do wish to see me again, I would not entirely be opposed to that. Maybe next time I will walk you to your room or to wherever it is an artist's assistant stays when he is in London. But, for now, I will just take home the thought of you."

Before climbing into the taxi, she places two of her fingers into my mouth. "I will be taking this from you for later when I need a little help drifting off to sleep."

RUFUS MONTGOMERY JR.

12

"WHAT THE FUCK DID I DO LAST NIGHT?" Stone buried his face into his pillow. "Did I really fuck the head of the CSI department, and in the house the murder took place? Fuck," he said, ending the reign of silence in his home.

He was pretty sure he came inside her too. Not only that, but he had worked his way through the drink's he had when he got home last night. He could still taste Hennessey, milkshake, and Ronda's pussy on his lips. Just another reminder that last night really happened. "Is it really only six o-clock?" He squinted at his phone still tethered to the wall by its charger. "Time to add coffee to all the things I've managed to put in my mouth in the last twenty-four hours. He sat on the edge of his bed. Ten minutes passed as he sat there and replayed the events of the day before. Could he have truly not left any evidence of himself in that house? What was he missing?

Dark Whisper: The Fire That Burns Within

The cold wood floors made Stone quickly step back onto the black carpet that his bed rested on. Sliding his feet into his house-shoes, he was now ready to move about. Shivering as the water dripped from his nose, he opened his eyes and watched as ripples moved away from the center of every droplet. Steam filled the room as the shower water heated up. Lifting his head up to find his mirror foggy, he reached for the tube of toothpaste and pulled a thick green layer over his toothbrush reminding him of Ronda's piercing green eyes. Getting in the shower and leaning his head back, he filled his mouth with water, and swished it around as the water flowed over his head and into his mouth. The taste of mint replaced the taste of Ronda as he washed what was left of her off his dick. How was he going to face her at work now? Things were already weird between them, and now this. She said he was her boyfriend. Did she mean by that? Was she serious or was she fucking with him again? He could never tell with her and her dark humor that probably came from spending so much time around dead people. After her goodnight text, everything else was a blur. He didn't even know she had his number. How the hell did she happen to get it? Today is going to be a fucking mess, Stone thought. They were looking for a killer and had no leads. In addition to that, he now had an acquired taste for the head of forensics' vagina.

Stone paused for a moment and thought back to the night before. Ronda's smile, her taste, everything about her was intoxicating. Did the killer feel the same hunger he did when he saw Ronda leaning over the island in that kitchen? When did his sexual hunger turn into his hunger to kill? Did he come there planning to kill her or was it a killing of opportunity, or sex games gone wrong ending with her death. This killer was seasoned. There was no doubt he had done this a time or two before.

The frigid air from the open refrigerator sent a chill through Stone. He was almost out of almond milk.

"WHY IS THIS THE ONE MORNING THAT TRAFFIC IS on my side? It's as if some evil force wants to see me suffer today. If there is a God, Keith takes a sick day today and I won't have to deal with him on top of everything else," Stone said.

It wasn't even eight yet and Stone was almost at the station. As he pulled in, he scanned the parking lot and as his luck would have it, Ronda's car was already there. She spent most of her time in the basement. Stone figured it would be a while before he ran into her. She should be down there poking at her dead friends. Keith, on the other hand, was always readily available. It's almost like he has been assigned Stone as punishment for some past sin.

Before Stone sees his desk, he heard a voice that confirmed he would be punished straight away. Ronda was sitting on his desk with her feet on his chair surrounded by the other officers. Keith was standing closest to her, taking all of it in about what he is now calling our case.

"Do we have the morning meeting at my desk now, or is it still being held in the bullpen?" Stone asked as he walked to his desk. "And no cookies this morning?"

"Your cousin didn't feel like baking last night. However, she was happy to hear that you still enjoy grandma's cookies, and that she got the recipe right." Jim shouted from his office where most of the time his door stayed open. He liked to try his best to stay a part of what went on outside what he called his prison.

"Here's your coffee, Stone." Keith presented Stone with a hot white cup with his name, Stone, written on the side.

Stone looked over at Ronda to find her wearing a knowing smile. He took a drink as both her and Keith look on in anticipation. "Shit, this is a great cup of coffee."

"You take it with almond milk, right?" Ronda's soft voice consumed the room. "I remembered." She still donned that creepy yet strangely cute smile.

"That is correct, Ms. Brice. I do take my coffee with almond milk." Stone tried to hurry past the conversation.

"Thought you would need it after the night you had," she added. "After leaving the house last night you said you needed a drink. I figured from not finding anything helpful at the scene you would be tying on a few."

"Oh, come on, Stone, you can call me Ronda." She looked at me like a woman that knew how it felt to have him inside her.

"You two were unable to find anything new?" Keith chimed in, and for the first time, Stone welcomed it. "What's our next move? It seems like the killer has left us nothing to go on. Maybe we should revisit the evidence we do have."

"What useful evidence do we have, Keith?" Ronda asked as she took her feet off Stone's chair, giving him permission to sit down. Her tight blue slacks did nothing to hide her lines. The modest T-shirt she wore proved that she did not have to try hard to be sexy. The red hair that held her face like two cupped hands, made it hard not to look at her beautiful green eyes.

Stone couldn't shake the thought of how her pussy felt on his lips. The taste of it, her very essence sent a shiver up and down his spine. He took another sip of his coffee and noticed a familiar taste on his coffee cup.

"Still enjoying your coffee, detective?" she asked, glancing down at her zipper.

"Best coffee I've ever had," he replied. "Must be the brand of almond milk you used. I may need to have you bring me in coffee every morning with that milk in it."

"How was your visit at the scene last night, Stone?" Jim asked.

RUFUS MONTGOMERY JR.

Stone almost choked on the hot liquid. How did they know they were returning to the house? How and what does he know? "What do you mean, captain?"

"Any new evidence from the cookie house? Keith texted me last night that you guys were going to take a second look at the house. Ronda didn't want to say anything until you made it in. Also, she was nice enough to bring you coffee. She said after the night you had you would need it. Now that you three are all here, can someone catch me up on things?

"We're planning to bring in her husband for more questioning." The only thing Stone got from that house last night was laid, and that in no way was going to help him solve the case.

"Her husband is already here," Keith whispered to Stone. "He came in shortly before you did. He asked for you by name."

"You did not think to start with that, Keith?"

"It's not the boys' fault," Ronda said as she slipped off Stone's desk. "I told him to let you have your coffee before bothering you with the details of the case." Her hand rubbed the back of his neck softly.

"So, where is he?" Stone asked Keith trying to not think about Ronda's soft touch. Stone quickly stood up before his cock betrayed him. "Where did you put him, and did he say anything to you?"

"I put him in interrogation room three. He didn't say anything, just asked to speak to you," Keith said as he followed closely behind Stone. "I did notice that he looked extremely upset."

"I would imagine so," Ronda chimed in. "He did just lose his wife. Moreover, look how he found her. Tied up, naked, wet, and proper fucked."

Keith slammed into Stone when he brought the procession to a stop.

"Keith, if you laugh with the crazy redhead, I will shoot you where you stand and call it a training accident."

"Yes, detective." Keith held back a chuckle.

"I'm the crazy redhead now?" Ronda asked. "You have to admit how she was found was a bit fucked up for a husband to find his wife."

"His soon to be ex-wife." Stone corrected her. "And who's to say it was not his way of killing her before she could walk away with half of everything? Who else would know the house well enough to make it look like no one was ever there?"

"That would be easy to say," Ronda said as she composed herself. "But I am sorry to say he is not our guy."

Stone turned to look at his two shadows. He looked at Ronda a bit confused to why she was even with them. "How is it that you are so sure that he had nothing to do with her death? There weren't any signs of a break in. Whoever it was had all the time in the world to clean the scene without needing to turn on any lights. Remember, no one saw lights or movement in the house. That would take some knowledge of the house. Not to mention he was the person that found the body." Stone put down a compelling list.

"All very true," Ronda agreed. "But there is a problem with your theory."

"What might that be, Miss Brice?"

"From what I saw of him that night, that man in interrogation room three is no freak. I've been at the job of reading people for some time, and I know a freak when I see one. A man who would kill a woman as he makes her come at the same time is not in that room. He may have some insight that could help us with this case but looking at him to be the killer would be a waste of our time."

With all that said, Keith could only squeeze out one question. "How is it that you can tell a freak when you see one?"

"If you two are done, interrogation room three." Stone paused and then took the folder from Ronda. "You two can watch from the observation room. It's clear that you just say the first thing that comes to mind."

"What's wrong with that, Stone?" Ronda asked, truly at a loss.

"Nothing," Stone said, "If you two were comedians." He left them to join the dead woman's husband in room three.

"Good morning, Mr. Harold." Stone motioned for him to remain seated. "I only assume that is your last name." Stone tried to set the mood. The sound of the metal chair scrapping across the rough floor made Mr. Harold's words hard to make out.

"What was that?" Stone asked, placing Ronda's folder on the cold gray table.

"That is correct," Mr. Harold repeated. "Her last name is still the same as mine. We were not yet divorced."

"How was that going?" Stone asked as he thumbed through Ronda's notes.

"How was what going?" Mr. Harold replied. "I don't understand."

Stone took a good look at the dead woman's husband. "Was your wife seeing anyone new that had the same access to your home as you did?" Stone asked.

"Not that I know of. But you can understand how me and my soon to be ex-wife would not engage in conversations of who we may or may not be seeing," Mr. Harold said as he straightened in his seat.

"You didn't know if your wife had a boyfriend or not, Mr. Harold?" Stone had a hint of asshole in his voice. "Would you say that you two still got on well in spite of the divorce?"

"We did not hate one another, if that's what you're asking." He rubbed his empty ring finger.

Detective Stone thought back to the night of the murder and remembered that finger with a ring on it. He recalled the next day in the morgue the woman's left hand had no signs of a ring. It was clear that she had removed her ring some time ago, where he was still holding on to hope. Quickly looking through the photos, Stone found the one with her left hand. As he recalled, there wasn't any tan lines where her wedding ring would have been. "If you two still got on well, what was the reason for the divorce?" Stone asked, conveniently leaving the folder open with the photo of her empty ring finger showing. "Would you say it was a mutual decision between the two of you?"

"Far from it," the scorned husband replied. "For me, it came out of nowhere. One day I thought everything was great. Next thing I knew Ella was telling me how unhappy she was and wanted to end our marriage. Imagine my shock."

Stone could see the man retreat into his thoughts. "I take it you were pretty angry when presented with this." Stone pushed just a bit more.

"No," Mr. Harold quickly responded. "I was more confused and hurt than anything else. I was blindsided. Like I said, I didn't see it coming."

"When did she stop wearing her ring?" Stone continued with the heavy questioning.

"What's with all the questions?" Mr. Harold lashed out, still unaware, rubbing his ring finger. "I'm not sure what's going on here, but I came in hoping you had some answers to what happened to my wife." His eyes narrowed. "You don't think I had something to do with what happened to her, do you?"

"Just trying to get a little look into her life before the night she was killed. Being her husband, you are a big part of that past we will need to take a look into." Stone said.

"Well, it sounded more to me like you were trying to build my motive. I came here seeking help not to be accused." He squared his shoulders. "Here is a look into her past; Ella hated raisins. I mean, she really hated those things. Those cookies must have been for someone else."

"How do you feel about raisins, Mr. Harold? Did you also have issue with them?"

"I love them, Detective Stone."

Stone leaned forward. "They very well could have been made for you then."

"No, sir." Mr. Harold sat back in the uncomfortable chair.

The two men stared at each other, waiting for the other to interrupt the silence that had taken over Interrogation Room Three.

"Please, explain to me how those cookies could not have been for you. You do enjoy raisins, do you not?"

"I do. However, I have a serious allergy to oatmeal. Ella would not have eaten them, and I can't have them. I know you have a job to do, detective, but you need to understand I loved my wife very much, and the last thing I would want is her dead. Yes, I was hurt when she asked for a divorce, but in hindsight, I should have seen something was wrong when she changed. She wanted different things, and I had to come to terms with that."

"Changed in what way?" Stone asked. "What was it that she wanted?" He saw the embarrassment in Mr. Harold's face.

His hand covered his mouth as if to try to hold back words he would rather not speak. "If you must know and if it will help in any way," he said. The words sounded thick as they left his mouth. "She started wanting to try new things in bed. At first, I found them fun and exciting. Then things became more intense and a bit out of my comfort zone. I've never been what people would call kinky. To tell you the truth, Ella is only the third woman I have even been with."

The vibration of Stone's mobile phone made him jump. It was Ronda.

RUFUS MONTGOMERY JR.

"Sorry, Mr. Harold, I have to check this."

Ronda: "I told you he was no freak! But you're still my bitch.

Stone could almost feel her making faces through the one-way glass. As the she-devil said, this man is no freak. Furthermore, he couldn't eat oatmeal.

"Truly, Mr. Harold." Stone folded his lips in and took a moment. "You have helped immensely. Please forgive my line of questioning, I have a job to do." Stone closed Ronda's folder with the photos of Ella. Stone stood up. "I really appreciate you taking the time to stop in and speak to us. If you remember anything that you think may help, please don't hesitate to call me." Stone put a card with all his information on it into Mr. Harold's hand.

"Thank you. I will put this with the first one you gave me." Mr. Harold placed the card into his left inner jacket pocket.

"One more question, if you don't mind," Stone asked.

Mr. Harold fixed his collar. "Of course. What is it?"

"You were the one who found the body, so you must still have a key to your home?"

"Yes, I do. As I told you, we still got on well and I would never come over without her knowing first. Several of my things are still there."

"Then, Mrs. Harold knew you were stopping by that night?"

"Yes, she did," he replied. "In fact, she was the one who asked me to. She had some paperwork she needed me to pick up."

"You stopping by was prearranged?" Stone tried to build a bit of a timeline and hoped Mr. Harold would let something slip.

"Actually, no, it was not prearranged."

"Then what was it?" Stone asked as he stepped from behind the table.

"I received a text from her to stop by. It seemed a little late to me, but her new single life sometimes kept her out. I just assumed she wanted me to have the paperwork before my busy week started on Monday."

"What is it that you do that keeps you so busy, Mr. Harold?" Stone asked.

RUFUS MONTGOMERY JR.

"I'm an architect. I've been working on that new art complex that's going up. We're on a bit of a time crunch trying to get it up and ready for a big exhibit they have coming."

They both turned when the door to the interrogation room suddenly opened. The look on the faces of Ronda and Keith had both the men a bit uneasy.

"Is that it?" Mr. Harold asked, trying to put it all together himself.

"Yes, that will be it. Officer Keith will show you out." Stone's voice broke the awkward encounter the two brought with them. "I think you met him that night and again this morning when you arrived."

"I did." Mr. Harold nodded.

"This young lady is the head of our CSI department." Stone handed Ronda the light brown folder.

"Sorry for your loss," Ronda said as she presented her right hand. "I am taking very good care of her, sir."

"Thank you." Mr. Harold closed his hand around hers. "I am sure you are, and I appreciate all that you guys are doing."

"Ms. Brice is the best we have, and if there is anything to be found in your house, she will find it," Detective Stone reassured the grieving husband. "Keith, please show our guest out."

"Are you going to stare at me until I tell you that you were right?" Stone asked, trying not to make eye contact with Ronda. "That text was very unprofessional, lady."

Ronda leaned in close and whispered, "You coming inside me was incredibly unprofessional, young man." She stepped back. "Let's just say that text makes us even."

"Tell me you got something other than him not being into freaky sex from that interview," Stone said. "Because other than taking himself out of the suspect pool he gave us little. I hope you saw something I missed. If so, please do not keep me waiting."

"Let's look at what we have." Ronda pulled up a nearby chair. "Whoever killed her knew she was living alone. Therefore, he must have been aware that she was going through a divorce and her husband wouldn't be there. He or she knew their way around, so they had to have been in the house before that night."

"Then we should canvas the neighborhood again with different questions," Stone said.

"Yes, they may have seen more than they realized," Ronda agreed. "Another thing we know is this person did not feel the need to hurry. Much time was put into cleaning the house just to fuck with us. They could have wiped away proof of them being there, but they also erased any trace of her presence."

"Why go through so much trouble to mess with the police?" Keith asked.

Stone looked back to see Keith standing over his right shoulder. "Because he's an asshole." Stone said as he wondered how long this awkward kid was standing over him. "Do I need to tie a bell to you, you ghostly fuck?" Stone said with a little laugh in his words. "This killer is definitely an asshole. That, I am sure of.

Ronda fingered through her papers. "There is something else we now know for sure." Ronda stopped on the part of her notes that showed the time of death.

"What else do we know for sure, Ms. Brice?" Keith asked.

"Unless Miss Harold sent that text from beyond, she wasn't the one who sent that text to her husband."

13

I FEEL THE MORNING WELL BEFORE MY room is filled with the proof that morning has arrived. The taste of her finger and mouthwash still lingers in my mouth—verification that last night was real. As I try to see if I can feel my face yet, my hands still smell like her hair. The plush curtains are like razor blades to the touch. Ripping them apart to let the morning in is the way I like to start my day in this city. Up before the city starts to breathe is the best part of the day. That time, and the time in the middle of the night when you know most humans are drifting away. In that time, I can finally be me. I no longer need to play human. I take it all in and feel my heartbeat slow, allowing myself to take in all the smells I had to let go ignored.

"Why the hell is it so cold in here?" I hear my own voice interrupting my train of thought. It's something when you try to shut yourself up. Is it that the two sides of my brain work too independently? Oh, well. Where did I leave my phones? It's only quarter past six, so I have about an hour before Stacy is calling or texting to see when I'll be starting my day. If she only knew how early I did start my day, she would start expecting too much from me. I prefer her see me as a lazy artist. Now, to take inventory: room keys, headphones, towel. If I'm lucky, I'll have the gym to myself again this morning. If someone is there, hopefully they will lack the desire to hold a conversation.

    I put my headphones on before I even leave the room. I like to shut the world out, because being a hunter means always being aware of what's going on around you. My trainers are laced, and I am ready to go. The air in the hallway warm and damp. It must have rained some overnight. So far, so good. I walk to the lift and encounter no one. Most people that check-in here are on some kind of business trip. On every turn, you could run into some rich asshole like my mate with the missing wallet. Got to watch myself with that one. I can see me coming on holiday to disappear him.

    It's been some time since I've done any work in London, like my main man, Jack the Ripper. He took this city for a ride.

Dark Whisper: The Fire That Burns Within

You may ask him why he did it, and what was the motive behind it all? Was it revenge for a wrong that had been done to him? Could it have been blood lust and the need to see the inside of all those women? Maybe he was just as they called him. Maybe he was pure evil and killed to spread fear in a city that became comfortable.

Sometimes I entertain the thought of it being a woman doing this, after she found the whore her husband visited. That always brought a beat of joy to me. It's mighty arrogant of men to claim death for themselves, but not think a woman could wield the same evil. That makes me laugh aloud. One thing I'll not do is underestimate the evil a woman is capable of.

Perfect. There's no one here to have to play nice with. Someone made it in before I did and left the smell of perfume and sweat. It is almost a pleasant aroma. By the pungency of her tang, she has not been gone long. I would say ten to twenty minutes at most. Timing is everything. It's a great tool for someone with my hobby. Now to go for a little run...

The sound of music and my heart beating in my head brings me to an almost hypnotic state. I still remember how sweet she smelled. The taste of her was amazing. I could never understand how her nipples tasted like sweet wine. She would always just say it was her little secret. I would kill to have one more taste of her, but I am always in control. So, instead, I killed her. The bit of her that had been left on the fingers of my glove, mixed with crumbs was a nice treat after all that cleaning. I could have pointed them to the husband, but that would have cleared up too fast and then they would be back to it. They would have to looked at him anyway. No worries. The confusion of absence of evidence will keep them spinning. You know what they say about idle hands. I don't mean to be an asshole, but I'm an asshole. She was something special—I may even miss her. Some of the things she wanted to try even had me taken aback at times. I wonder if she realized what was happening to her, or did she take it for another game? She did enjoy herself till the bitter end. That's the wettest I've ever seen her get. That is probably why there was so much of her left on my glove. It was almost as if she were baked into the cookie. Her flavor mixed with the sweet of the raisins made for a perfect blend.

I need to keep an eye on the time. Wouldn't want to miss Stacy's call. I read her texts and left them unanswered. Most of the times I don't mean to do it, but boy does it drive her crazy.

The line between who works for whom is mostly blurred in our relationship.

The temperature in the room changes as soon as she opens the door.

Clank!

Sounds from the weights meeting drowns out the loud click the gym door makes when it closes. She is dressed different, but I remember her from our brief encounter. She's got a goofy walk, but her ass is pleasant to look at. Just a few more and I will leave her to it. Hopefully, she did not pay as much attention to me as I did her yesterday. It's five till seven. I have time for ten more. Plus, I am enjoying watching her stretch. If I ever met the person who invented yoga-pants, I would kiss them on the lips. The way it hugs her shape and shows off all the parts of her that brings about imagination. I should be on my way, don't want to miss my wake-up call.

"I'm not truly that forgettable, am I?" she asked as I passed her on the elliptical.

I almost made it to the door. "Not at all, I just thought women would rather to be left alone when they worked out." I tried to work out where her accent was from. "I figured if you wanted to speak, you would, and here you are saying something." I am going to miss that call for sure now.

"A woman doesn't want to be bothered at the gym until she wants to be bothered at the gym," she said, pulling one of her ear buds out and tossing it over her shoulder. Her awkward smile was cute and painful at the same time. "And I would very much like to be bothered by my hero."

Wait, is she trying to be seductive? Man is she missing the mark. "Hero?" I do not know what this crazy woman is talking about.

"Yesterday, on the lift. If not for you I might still be wandering this hotel looking for my room. You were on the lift. My hero."

Hero? More like killer that could have very well left you in your tub with a pair of open wrists and a room with a story to tell. "I am glad I was there when you needed my assistance. Fifth floor, right?" I try my best to reassure her that she's not forgettable. "Where is your accent from, if you do not mind me asking?" She has my attention now. But question is, does she really want it?

Dark Whisper: The Fire That Burns Within

Still working the coordinating silly smile and seductive voice, she sees my question as an opportunity to play. "Where would you place my accent?"

She is becoming more interesting. She's got thick, curly maroon hair along with adorable freckles. "I will go out on a limb and say Irish born? But I also would say you did some traveling as a child and picked up a bit from the places you landed. There is even a little Aussie twang in some of your words." By the look on her face, either I got it right or I have offended the shit out of her.

"How did you do that?" She asks as her pace slows on the elliptical. "No one ever gets it."

"Get what?"

"That I am Irish. And if they even make that out, they never pick up that I spent time in Australia. How did you do that?" She stands there looking deep into my eyes. It's making me very uncomfortable.

"I really should be on my way." My voice shatters the silence. "Plus, I'm disturbing you. Enjoy your workout, and it was nice seeing you again." I start walking to the exit.

RUFUS MONTGOMERY JR.

"Nancy," she says right before that loud click of the door opening.

I pause a moment before I say anything. "Jason," I reply. "Nice to have met you, Nancy." As I move through the threshold, Nancy has more to add.

"Since we seem to keep similar hours, maybe you and I could catch breakfast one morning?"

"That would be delightful, Nancy. Again, enjoy your workout." The door makes its second click as it closes behind me. As I go to my room, I can see the hotel has come alive. The Concierge is in her forest green blazer. Freshly made coffee steams in a mug as that aroma fills the room. From the hotel kitchen, the head chef tells the morning cooks that breakfast is minutes away and he will not be late. I can see the door attendant through the frosted doors sweeping the steps and wiping down the little statues that keep his company day after day. He takes pride in his station, and it shows. The walk from the gym is not a long one, but there is a lot to see. There are others walking to the gym. Some don't notice me. People spend a great deal of time not looking up. Either they are checking who has liked their last post, or they are making the world aware of what they are doing. For many, there's a desire to be famous for no other reason than you have an opinion. There's that constant need to show everyone how interesting your non- interesting life is. If everyone knows what you are doing, that makes it much more interesting.

Looks to me that I left just in time to beat the exodus of people posting "Working On My Fitness," on their social media of choice. We all know that person.

So far, I have managed to make it to the lift without having to hold a meaningless small talk, but I am late for my wakeup call from Stacy. It will be the normal barrage of verbal abuse on how I should get my day started earlier. Standing in the hallway in front of my room door, I can hear my phone vibrating on the hard surface of the nightstand. I get in just in time to miss the last rattle.

I dial her back and listen to the phone ring. I know she's holding her phone watching my name flash.

"Glad to see you're up. Did you enjoy yourself last night?" Stacy asks, sounding like she knows more than I would like her to. It's a little thing she enjoys doing when she thinks I'm off my game.

RUFUS MONTGOMERY JR.

"Excuse me?" I ask. I'm not saying much until I have a better idea of what she may know. "I'm just getting up, so you're going to have to be a little clearer about what you're talking about until I'm fully awake." I'm trying to buy myself a little time to catch up with her sneaky ass.

"You told me you had a thing last night," she says. "I was just wanting to know how that went. I do hope it had something to do with you getting some work done for upcoming projects.

"Yes, and no. But I may have found some inspiration for future work."

"Your server texted me last night," she says, almost in passing.

"My what?" Is she still messing with me?

Stacy sighed. She was clearly annoyed by my response. "The server girl from lunch yesterday that you gave my number to."

"Oh, her. What did she want?" I want the hear her say it.

"Apparently you were right—she's into you." Her voice is filled with the contempt.

"I think she is more interested in finding out if your vagina is as delightful as I had mentioned," I say.

"On the phone with you for less than five minutes and you manage to work my pussy into a conversation." I can almost hear a smile on her face. "Isn't it a bit early to have the mention of my pussy on your lips?"

"Stacy, it is never too early to have your pussy on my lips." I brace myself for her reply.

"Never too early for you to start being a dick, I see." Stacy replies, her words by no means disappoint. "Anyway, your server texted to see if we were available to hang out with her and her friends last night. I had already laid down to a good book, and I remembered you told me you already had plans, whatever the hell that could have been."

"So, what did you tell her?" I ask. I still have plans for that one. "Were you nice to our new friend?"

"Yes, I was nice to your little victim. I told her you would get back to her when we were both available to hang out. Then…" Stacey pauses, her hesitation piques my interest.

"Then what Stacy?" I ask, taking the bait.

RUFUS MONTGOMERY JR.

Stacy being Stacy reminds me I'm not in charge. "I don't hear Frank Sinatra playing, so you haven't started your morning yet." She answers but doesn't answer. "You remember we have to meet with Benjamin and the others at the gallery later this morning, right?" The tone of her voice makes it clear that she was not going to answer my question about our server until she was good and ready. "I would appreciate it if you were not late. You know how I hate being alone with that prick. He's always pestering me to put him in direct contact with the artist. We both know the boss's thoughts on doing that."

"Well let me go and put on a little Blue Eyes and get this started." The extra time in the gym set me back a bit, and I do want to make a stop before going to the gallery. "No worries, you will have your assistant there with you, doing what a good assistant does."

Stacy laughs. "Let's just be happy they think you're a little slow. You know I keep you around for a pretty face and a hard dick? Otherwise, they would have real questions."

"Why do you say that?"

"If you haven't noticed, you are a shit assistant. I mean, fucking bad. If I didn't know you better, I would think you should be on some Adderall or something." Stacy happily spells out what she meant, leaving me no closer to understanding what part was intended to hurt my feelings.

"But, Stacy, you told me before that I should be on something to keep me from wondering off back into my own thoughts."

"Yes, I guess I have," she says leaving it at that. After listening to her, I decide I should really get started.

I go through my playlist and let it play. "Sounds to me like you are already ahead of me, so I have some catching up to do if I am to make it there in time to save you. I'll even pick you up a raisin bagel and a coffee when I get mine."

"See what I mean?" she says. "I don't eat that shit, and if you bring me one, I will kill you with it. A halfway decent assistant would know what I take for breakfast, a shitty assistant would not."

I hear the phone hang up. "Oh well. I'll just do it my way."

```
Good morning. Hope you slept well.
—Jason
```

RUFUS MONTGOMERY JR.

"Shower time." I still have so much yet to do.

"I WILL HAVE TWO COFFEES—ONE BLACK, THE OTHER with almond milk and sugar."

"Name?" The barista asks.

"Jason, but I have more to add to that order."

"Ok, go ahead with the rest." The barista clicks his pen.

"I also want two teas—both with almond milk, one with sugar."

"Will that be it?" he asks.

"I will take two cinnamon raisin bagels with just a touch of cream cheese on them, and that will be it." Did Stacy say yes or no on that bagel? I really should pay more attention to her when she talks.

I'm still trying to figure out if my feelings should be hurt or not, or what the proper response should be if they were. Oh, and there was the matter of what shoes should I wear today.

Guess I'll just figure it out when I get there, as I always do. Man does this guy smell great. I think I've killed a woman that wore the same perfume.

"I said fucking half and half, this tastes like milk! What did you not understand about half and half?" A familiar voice engulfs the hotel coffee shop. "Make it again!" he shouts, followed by the sound of a splash.

"I am very sorry, sir," a gentle-voiced barista replies, "I will have it remade for you, right away."

I get a better look at the man. It's my mate from the lobby yesterday. If I keep running into this dick, I may have to make this a working holiday.

"Please step over to the other counter to pick up your order, sir." The barista points to where my "friend" is berating the other worker.

"Perfect. Call me Jason." I smile at him.

"Okay. Here is your change, Jason," the sweet-smelling barista replies.

His hands look soft as cotton balls. "Keep the change, my friend. I need to say hello to a mate of mine."

RUFUS MONTGOMERY JR.

"Don't tell me you're mates with that man. He's bloody awful." You could hear the disappointment in his voice.

"Friends?" I should clear this up before I am dubbed an ass by association. "I would not call what we are friends. I was using that term loosely. In fact, you may like him a little more than I do." Hearing that made him laugh as he put a fist filled with colorful money and coins into the tip jar.

"Well, in that case, whatever hello you have planned for him, give him one for me."

If he only knew he's made himself an accomplice, he would maybe take that back. "Will do. I will give him a hello from you as well."

The color leaves the asshole's face when he looks to his left and sees me walking his way. It's almost enough to know the lasting effect I have left on him. The smug way he stood there before he saw me makes me want to grab a fist full of straws and see how far I could push them through his neck. Tap him for blood the same way they would tap a tree for sap. Would everyone be appalled, or would I receive a standing ovation for killing this simpleminded fuck wearing a thousand-dollar black

Italian suit does not make him look any less a wanker from where the girl who is helping him stands.

"You must forgive my friend." I watch as a horrified look creeps onto his face. "Have you gotten that financial situation dealt with?" Waving my wallet at him is a fun added touch. Maybe he'll be the first person I kill using the power of embarrassment. Oh, he looks angry, not embarrassed. He will probably die from anger. My face hurts. Is this what happiness feels like? I'm smiling so hard I can hardly speak. "Listen, if he's having problems paying for his breakfast, I assure you, he is good for it. You should see the expensive billfold he has. Show it to her. Shit, I was impressed when I saw it pressed against the inside of that rubbish bag."

"How the bloody hell did you get that?" The surprise in his gray eyes almost makes the young girl remaking his coffee spill it on herself.

"Careful now, don't want you to have to make a third cup." She gets the jest when I give her a playful wink. It's clear he doesn't have any respect for the working class, and he most certainly doesn't hold any for women. As a man with as many sisters as I have, I will not stand for this. I publicly shame him, which for him, is better than the alternative. "Certainly, from his suit and this extremely nice billfold, he is a very important and busy man." I hand him back his wallet. "You really should keep this somewhere else. You make it far too easy for someone who may mean you injury."

"Injury?" he says, pulling free from my embrace. "Who are you?"

"Come now. Just yesterday I was going to loan you some money to get you out of your hardship." I've been told my smile can bring someone to great anger. As he stands there almost frozen, looking at my smiling face, I see rage building in his face. His face goes from pale white to Victoria Secret thong red.

"I bloody told you I was in no need of your money you…" He pauses as he looks around.

"Here is your coffee, sir," says the small barista. "Half and half, no milk. Just like you asked. Sorry for the mix up."

Still unable to whip that wicked smile off my face, I give my friend some more good advice. "You should go. Wouldn't want you to be late for whatever it is you do. Don't you worry—I will leave this young lady a tip for you. Word is, you give shit tips anyway."

He takes his freshly made coffee and shuffles past me.

"Twenty quid?" the small barista asks as she looks at the money on the counter. "You really don't have to." She pushes the bill back at me.

"Oh, but I didn't. He did." I give her another playful wink. "He should really put that billfold somewhere harder to get to."

"Here you are, Jason, two coffees and two cups of tea, and two raisin bagels, light on the cream cheese."

"Thank you so very much, my man. I have another twenty quid here for you. It's almost like they're falling from a prick's wallet." I turn to leave, but I have to ask, "How the hell do you smell so good? You have to tell me its name. I want to get some for my boss. She would love it."

As I approach the grand glass doors, like always, the attendant stands ready to great me. His shiny black leather gloves make a sound when it's stretched. Furthermore, how he remembers everyone's name is beyond me. "Good morning, mister..."

"I told you to just call me Jason. You and I both work with our hands, so no need for that Mr. business." I cut him off before he can finish. "How are you doing this morning? Are you keeping warm out here?"

"Just marvelous, Jason." Here he is out in the elements and marvelous. Then there are those who complain of having milk instead of half and half in their coffee. "The cold doesn't bother me none. I'll take this over the rain any day if I were to be given a choice."

"I concur. This UK rain laughs at the sight of umbrellas. At least when it snows it only comes from one direction." From my couple of days here I have found him more than the others truly worth stopping to talk to. "Well, Paul, I must be going. By the way, I told them in the hotel restaurant when you stop in for lunch to charge it to my room. Also, I already ordered you the soup. I had it two nights ago for room service. It was delicious, and I figured it would be something you might enjoy." I hold both my hands up a bit. "I would shake your hand, Paul, but..."

"No worries, Jason. You have a good day."

14

GOOD MORNING, SORRY I TOOK SO LONG TO get back to you. Got a late start. And yes, I did sleep well. Thank you—Vicky

As Vicky pressed send, she heard, "No puddle this morning?" She took a moment to turn around. She did not want him to see the smile on her face. That would give away how happy she was to hear his voice.

"Bloody stalker, I see. I've never had one of them," Vicky replied sheepishly.

"A stalker with coffee and snacks," Jason said with a paper bag accompanying his jest.

Vicky turned to find him standing there with a grin that either makes you want to kiss him or kill him. Holding a cup holder with four cups with steam still rising from them in one hand and the bag he shook at her. He stood looking like a child waiting to see if he would be allowed to go out and play.

"I take it that you weren't sure how I take my coffee, or if I even drink coffee," Vicky said as people walked awkwardly between them. "Let me guess, two coffees and two teas." She walked over to him and stood there facing him. The London Eye was behind him. Loud cars passed by, and yet, all they saw and heard was each other.

"Now who's the stalker?" Jason brought the cups down to where she could read the labels. "I don't recall seeing you in the coffee shop. But of course, you were probably crouched down behind something." He leaned over and kissed Vicky on the top of her head.

"What would I have seen if I was watching you this morning on your coffee run?" She asked as she left him still wondering if he got one right. "Who are you when no one is looking, Jason?"

Jason's eyes gave away nothing. "If you were there, you would see how much of a nice guy I was. You would see how good a tipper I am." He wore a devilish smirk. "Also, you would have seen this barista that I swear to the God smelled like hope and Heaven itself. I tipped him twice."

Vicky giggled as she held Jason's wrist and grabbed the tea with almond milk and sugar. "America would have us think you guys are bad tippers." She looked at Jason and drank him down with her eyes.

Knowing what she meant, Jason laughed. "Like I told you when we first met, I am a bit of something else."

After setting down her large satchel, she placed two fingers in Jason's pocket and gently pulled. "Walk me to the tube, stalker, I have to get to work. You're going to make me late." She took a sip of her tea.

"I recall you saying you got a late start. How am I to blame for your impending tardiness?" Jason asked. "Did I not save you from that puddle this same time yesterday?"

"Yes," she replied. "My tardiness yesterday was also your fault." She took another sip.

Jason now dawned a look of confusion. "But…"

"You're pretty. Don't try and put it all together. Now pick up the pace."

Vicky pulled on his pocket once more. Jason smiled, did as he was told, and wondered how her short legs carried her as fast as they did. He walked a few steps behind her so to get a better look at her ass in the light blue pants that hugged her figure so well. "What will you do with the other three cups?" She asked, still keeping the pace.

"I take my coffee with almond milk and sugar, and I think my boss takes her coffee black."

"So, you are telling me you don't know exactly what your boss drinks?" Vicky asked.

Jason shrugged. "Not exactly."

Vicky stood there looking at him as one would look at a puppy in a sweater. "Sounds to me like you're a shit assistant." Her words were filled with affection. "This is where we go our separate ways. Last I checked, you go the other way." She motioned her head in the other direction.

"Now who's stalking whom?" Jason said, twisting his lips like a kid feigning innocence.

Vicky examined his face. "Does that work with anyone?"

Jason nodded. "More often than you would think, little lady."

"Well, I watched you to make sure your cheeky foot grabbing ass wasn't following me." She took another sip. "And cream next time."

"Excuse me?" Jason raised an eyebrow.

She shook the cup. "What weirdo drinks almond milk?" She looked him up and down as if to take a photo of him. "Now, if you would, then be on your way." Vicky leaned her head back and presented her lips to him. She could almost feel the smile on his as they touched hers. "On your way, yummy brown stalker man." Off she went.

Heat gently coursed through her cheek as she descended steps leading her under the city. Leaving both the embrace of the cold and his lips behind her, she thought back to them both. Her large satchel that doubled as a purse and briefcase hit her right leg every step she took. Vicky would constantly adjust it to keep it from ending up hitting her knees.

"Don't tell me you got up in time to stop for tea before work, young lady?" The casually dressed woman asked. Her hair hung almost to her waistline and was loosely braided. The streaks in her hair almost matched the purple shirt she wore. Her jeans were ripped at the knee, exposing her long thin legs to the elements, and she wore yellow Converse. She stood there examining Vicky's face for any clues.

"Not exactly." Vicky replied, trying to keep a straight face.

"What exactly do you mean, not exactly?" The woman moved in for a closer look at Vicky's face, looking for a hint of some kind. The tube roared up to the platform and allowed Vicky to break free from the stare.

"Oh, look, here's our ride. We should hurry if we're to get a seat." Vicky smiled as she adjusted her satchel and shuffled through the open doors.

The woman bit her bottom lip. She followed Vicky and sat next to her for the thirty-minute ride. They were accompanied by some of the other regulars that shared their tube. There's the businessman who never looked up from his phone. On occasion, he treated the tube like his own personal office, and yelled at people on the phone about something they forgot to include in some paperwork or the other. If they were to guess, he was a lawyer. Then there was the woman that Vicky and her traveling companion dubbed the "Prom Date." She always looks like she was overdressed for whatever she had planned for the day. One time she even got on with what they both decided had to be a wedding dress. The trainers she wore were a nice touch to her ensemble.

"How long do you plan to keep me waiting?" Vicky's friend asked, still curious as to why the change in Vicky's morning routine.

"Keep you waiting on what?" Vicky asked, trying to look unaware. "Was I in the middle of a story of some kind?" She sipped on her tea.

"Let me see if I have learned anything from you." Vicky's travel mate rubbed her chin like she wore a large beard.

"Okay, Karen, let's see what you've picked up from me." Vicky turned to face her.

She was still stroking her imaginary beard. "Before we get started, there needs to be some rules to keep you honest, of course."

"Yes of course, Karen. To keep me honest." The two women laughed.

"Nothing too difficult." Karen assured her. "You just need to confirm if I am correct or not."

Vicky smiled. "That seems fair enough. You may begin."

RUFUS MONTGOMERY JR.

Still having a go at the beard that hadn't yet come in, Karen started. "As long as I've been riding this tube with you, you've always managed to make it to the platform minutes, sometime seconds before the tube arrives. There was that month that I was sure you had died because you were so late you had to take the later tube."

Vicky nodded. "I remember that. It was a bit awkward when I came back and saw how close you and that old guy who did die became in my absence. How easily I had been replaced." Vicky shook her head.

"He was funnier than you, and on time." Karen teased. "We both know there is no way you somehow drug your ass out of bed this morning of all mornings with enough time to stop for a cup of tea. Therefore, I can only deduce that someone must have provided you with that hot yummy beverage. Also, I would hate to think you would stop for tea and not think to bring your longtime friend one as well. That would mean the old man was right about you."

"Hey," Vicky interrupted. "What did the old bastard say about me?"

"Don't speak ill of the dead." Karen rolled her eyes upward.

"You going to get on with it?" Vicky asked, waving her hand in front Karen's face.

"Yes, I am saying someone bought you tea and met you with it. Am I correct?" Karen waited for confirmation.

"You would be correct with your theory. Someone did purchase me this hot beverage," Vicky confirmed.

"Is this bringer of hot beverages an old acquaintance or a new one?" Karen asked.

"That would be a new friend," Vicky replied. "When did you become so forthcoming, Karen?" Vicky was becoming more impressed with Karen's dedication to her invisible beard.

Karen stopped and gave Vicky a once over. "How did I become so forthcoming? When I saw your slutty ass kissing on that cup of hot chocolate."

"Karen," Vicky said and then paused. "I thought this was a slut shaming free zone." They both laughed drawing attention to themselves.

"Was that the guy you told me about yesterday morning?" Karen asked.

RUFUS MONTGOMERY JR.

"Yes, that was him," Vicky said from behind her cup.

"Now you're kissing the cheeky foot guy? Don't tell me you spent the night with him. I could only imagine all the kinky foot sex stuff he was into." She paused. "Was he into kinky foot sex?" Karen twirled her feet around, her shoelaces flapped about.

"No," Vicky quickly replied.

"No, he wasn't into foot sex?" Karen asked, sounding a bit disappointed.

"We did not have sex of any kind. We just went out for a late dinner and some drinks. That was all, you freaky bitch."

Karen shrugged her shoulders. "What? You haven't lived till you've had a good toe sucking." She waved her Converses around.

Vicky wore a look of disgust on her face. "I know someone that can help you," she said as she pushed Karen's legs down.

"No, thanks," Karen replied. "I get my therapy from you on our rides to work. But, enough about me—how was the date? What does he do for a living?"

"From what little we talked about it; I think he's into art in some way. We did not talk too much about that." Vicky tried to think back to what had been said about what he did for a living.

"Did you tell him what you do for a living?" Karen asked.

"Not exactly," Vicky said, "it gets strange when you tell someone you spend your days looking at files filled with the details of violent acts committed by violent people to determine their reasoning behind it. Not only that, but sometimes I interview some of these same people to see if I can get into their heads and figure out what makes them work. No, I did not tell him what I do. I've found that to be a surefire way to get someone to stop being themselves. Except for maybe you." Vicky stopped to look Karen up and down. "You are like crazy hiding in plain sight."

"Don't know how to be any one but myself," Karen bragged, "but did you do that thing you do?"

"Did I read him?" Vicky asked. "I tried not to."

"So, you did." Karen now hung there waiting for Vicky's next words.

"Okay, maybe just a little." Vicky smiled.

"And?" Karen asked.

A hint of confusion accompanied her voice. "He seemed normal. Even though we only met yesterday, he made me feel comfortable around him." Vicky pulled on her ear. "Come to think of it he seemed to have had that effect on everyone around him."

"What are you saying, Vicky? He could be a psycho killer?" Karen asked as she looked at Vicky's cup suspiciously.

"No." Vicky laughed and offered the reluctant Karen a sip of her beverage. "Jason was very sweet, and truly a likeable person whose personality makes everyone drawn to him."

"Is he from around here?" Karen pressed for more information.

"Actually, no," Vicky replied. "I think he is from America."

"You think he's American. Either he's from America or he's not." Karen insisted.

"Not the way he put it." Vicky tried to clear things up. "When I made the observation that he was American, he said, "not quite." He said he was something else."

"What the fuck does that even mean?" Karen twisted her lips.

Vicky thought for a moment before she answered. "I noticed a bit of an accent when he was comfortable and after a few drinks. He hides it well, but when the subject of him came up, some of his words betrayed him. At some point he sounded like us with his choice of words."

Karen nodded her head as she took in all she had just heard. When she finally seemed to have worked it all out, she leaned forward. "What you're saying is he did not try to have kinky, sticky foot sex with you?"

Vicky, who had just taken a sip of her tea, struggled not to spit it out. After managing to hold it together, she gave her replied, "Glad to see you stuck to the important parts of the conversation."

Karen sat back proudly and threw her long right leg over her bony left knee. "See, I am getting the hang of this."

"Looks like your thirty minutes are up again." Vicky adjusted her satchel and stood up. "Here comes my stop." She grabbed the cold bar above Karen with her left hand. "Cold," she muttered under her breath.

RUFUS MONTGOMERY JR.

As the tube slowly came to a full stop, its doors started to creep open. "Go out there and keep us safe from psycho killers, Vicky," Karen said as she always did when her travel mate got to her stop.

"I will try," Vicky replied, then added, "Break a leg today."

Everyone left on the tube shook they're heads. Even the businessman took notice and looked up from his phone.

"I am not an actor," Karen said. "Not a good thing to tell a dancer, Vicky." Karen shouted.

Vicky smiled as she heard Karen's voice squeeze free from the closing tube doors. As Vicky approached the stairs that lead up to the city, she took one last sip. She smiled at the smell of him still on her hand. She threw away the cup and started her ascension for the world waiting above.

15

AS STACY ENTERED THE GALLERY, SHE COULD hear talking coming from the back corner of the large, empty building. Her every step added to the echo. Each stride she made described her bodies movements. She took pride in her shoes, and they spoke to the mood she happened to be in that day. They were her comfortable shoes for days she had to take things as they came. Even the shoes she purchased for running had personalities all their own.

    Stacy was not in any rush to deal with Benjamin, or as he has her call him, "Mr. Nat," and his bullshit this early in the morning. She took time to show herself around the gallery imagining Jason's paintings hanging on the walls. The rare opportunity to do this without Mr. Nat invading her thoughts with his opinion, she found peaceful. As long as those voices were just background, she could take this time to herself. She

RUFUS MONTGOMERY JR.

envisioned Jason's painting, entitled "My Place of Rest" hanging on this tall broad gray pillar shown by a soft white light from above. This painting was one where Jason played with the thought of mortality. A faded gravestone with a barely readable name was scribbled into the stone. You could just make out what she could only assume is his real name. There are only two in that collection, the second one just as abstract.

 Not all of his paintings were shadowed with so much gloom, but his favorites all seemed to be a bit on the dark side. He claimed those paintings that landed on to the canvas when he listened to the whispers. Some of them, even in their beauty, left her a bit uneasy, but somehow brought in the most when placed on sale. Never underestimate people's desire to hang death on their walls.

 Listening to Jason when speaking to potential buyers about the paintings and them having no idea he's responsible had always been amazing to Stacy. The first time she saw this, she thought for sure Jason was going to kill a buyer that could not stop going on about how much of a pompous ass the artist must be and claimed that he had seen him before. By the end of that gallery show, that man overpaid for every piece of work

Jason sold him and could not wait to get those paintings on his wall.

Jason's way with people always made her curious to how someone so detached from human emotions knew how to keep everyone around him engaged. It's almost like they were looking right at him and could only see what he allowed them to. Stacy wondered if she had seen the real him, or was she under the same spell the others were and didn't know it? She felt that she knew him better than most, but what did that even mean? When she started to feel like they were becoming close, and when they were alone, she would sometimes see him break character. But after that death in his family, whoever it was that she saw never returned when he did. It was as if that part of him was buried along with that family member. He had yet to tell her whom it was he lost, and she never knew how to bring that up to him. He still spoke of his mother however strange that relationship was. As for his father, Jason worked hard to be nothing like him, but even harder to be worthy of something given to him by his father.

Benjamin was the kind of person Jason would do everything in his power to not be around, if at all possible, yet from where she stood, they looked like best friends. Who was Jason when no one is looking?

"Good morning, Mr. Nat. I hope Jason isn't making any promises our boss hasn't approved." Jason always found it funny making her look like a bad person. "Hey Stacy, we've been waiting for you." Jason looked like a kid whose mother just came to pick him up from school.

"I picked you up some coffee," Jason said, as he shoved half a bagel in his mouth. Now with a free hand, he picked up one of the cups. What is that in his mouth?

"Help him," Benjamin instructed Tabatha even though he was in a better position to help than her. "Can't you see his hands are full?"

"Yes sir," Tabatha replied not entirely sure in what way she could help Jason.

"What do you have there, Jason? Did you pick me up coffee and a bagel?" Stacy asked. "Look, Tabatha, he just realized he can't answer me with his mouth full."

Tabatha giggled and tried not to look over at Jason. "Are you going to hit him later for that?" Tabatha asked gleefully.

Jason poked his bagel at Tabatha.

"Help him with that," Benjamin insisted.

"I told you not to say anything, Tab." Jason scolded her as he chewed the piece of bagel in his mouth.

"Not to say what, Tabatha?" Stacy inquired.

Almost bouncing off her feet, Tabatha started repeating Jason's earlier story.

"Shhhh," Jason loudly interrupted causing Tabatha to drop the half-eaten bagel.

"Will you stop terrorizing this woman?" Stacy turned to the prick. "Good morning, Mr. Nat."

"Good morning, Stacy," Benjamin replied. The weather outside was warmer than his greeting to her. "Come, let me show you what your assistant and I came up with for the upcoming show." He looked back to see if she was behind him. "Will the artist be joining us at this show?"

"What did you agree to?" Stacy asked Jason as soon as she thought her whispers to him would go unheard. "Tell me that isn't a fucking raisin bagel in there for me."

"I didn't promise him anything, but I did get him to buy that one drawing that you wanted in this show," Jason bragged. "You said you would kill for a raisin bagel."

"You truly don't listen to me, do you?" she said. "I said I would kill you with it if you brought me one of those nasty bagels you eat."

"That's why I brought you coffee. The bagel is for Tab," Jason said.

"Who eats that rubbish?"

"Fuck." Jason turned to find Tabatha standing there. "I will tie bells to your nipples if you don't start making more noise, I swear to God." Tabatha crossed her arms. "You couldn't have just eaten it for a fellow assistant?"

"You're a shitty assistant," Tabatha said as she took Stacy's coffee and left him with the unwanted baked goods. "Here you go Stacy."

"Thank you, Tabatha." Stacy happily took the hot drink. "Benjamin better be careful. I may just take you from him." She took a sip. "At least he got this right."

Jason leaned in close. "Really, Tab? You could've just said the bagel was yours."

"Why would I do that?" Tabatha smiled an awkward but cute smile. "I'm trying to take your job—my boss is a proper wanker. Probably why you two get along so well." She stepped up to keep pace with Stacy.

Jason stayed back for a moment and saw little Tabatha differently than usual. He caught himself and wiped that special smile he sometimes donned off his face. To him, this was not the place or time for that.

"Before you arrived, your assistant talked me into giving your boss more wall space." Benjamin pointed to the mapped layout of the gallery. "This way, you won't be sharing space with any other artists."

Stacy turned and looked at Jason. What the hell did he promise this freak? Jason painted, and she did the heavy lifting. "How exactly did Jason convince you of this?" Stacy asked. This was no doubt like the time he worked out a deal with a prince that had a thing for braiding hair. It would not have been that bad if he didn't need to be naked to braid her hair. Still, she didn't have to do her hair for two weeks so, there was that.

"Nothing to worry your pretty little head about." Benjamin winked at Jason. "Jason already texted your boss and got the okay."

"Oh, did he now?"

RUFUS MONTGOMERY JR.

"That job is as good as mine," Tabatha murmured under her breath.

Stacy's scarf blew over her coffee cup keeping her from taking that drink she was attempting. Benjamin pulled up his collar and turned to see the others already looking at the door.

"Sorry, did I let the cold in." Her voice added to the chill. "Is this where the show's going to be next week?" She let the door close slowly behind her.

"Can I help you?" Benjamin walked past Stacy and the others. "What have you heard about the upcoming show? Only avid collectors have been invited to this event. Who are you?" Benjamin extended a sweaty hand to her.

She smiled and shook it. "I represent one of those collectors you speak of." Her green eyes panned the room, looking on the walls as if they were already covered in art.

"You must have great knowledge of art," Benjamin sounded impressed. "Did you study art?"

"No," she replied, reclaiming her hand. "Law." Her attention was now fixed on Stacy.

"What makes you qualified to decide what art is good art?" Stacy's words were covered with a hint of thorns.

"For one, I have eyes, and two, my clients seem to think I am. Isn't that what really matters?" She turned her attention to Stacy. "Deni." She extended a hand to Stacy.

"I'm Stacy, and this is…"

"I know this hero," Deni said with honey in her voice. "We met the other day."

"Hero?" Tabatha looked at Jason as if he had something on his face. "This guy? What did he help you find, your bloody vibrator?" Tab took her time checking this woman out. She was dressed modestly fitting for the weather. Black jeans, brown leather boots, white sweater, and a brown leather jacket that fell a little past her thighs. Her blond hair and haunting green eyes caused Tabatha to stare.

"The other day?" Stacy said.

"Yes, Stacy." Jason joined in the odd encounter. "The other morning when I was on my way to meet you at Benjamin's building to go over the paintings."

"And … the hero thing?" Tabatha asked.

"Yes, Tab, I kept a man from stepping in front of a lorry," Jason explained his heroic deed. "Deni, is it?" Jason asked, making the excuse to take a better look at her. With all that was going on with the man showing such gratitude he never got the chance to take in much more than those eyes of hers.

"It's Deni." She shook her head. "And you're Jason?"

"It's Jason, yes." He turned back to Tabatha. "Deni was there and saw it all."

Tabatha adjusted her glasses. Jason's voice seemed a touch not like the Jason she was used to.

"You said you know this artist?" You could practically see Benjamin's mouth water at the thought of getting more information.

"Yes," she said. He seemed to annoy her. "The main artist you're showcasing. I've wanted to see more of his most recent works. From the ones I have seen, his style has changed a bit since the death of his grandmother."

"His grandmother?" Stacy thought this woman clearly knew more than she apparently knew. "I don't know if I mentioned, but Jason and I both work for the artist and there has been no mention of you."

"Well, if you work for him you must know how closed off he is from those around him. There is no surprise that he has not mentioned me," Deni said.

"Those three symbols he signs his paintings with," Benjamin said, "what do they mean?" He tried to work in as many questions as he could between Stacy and this Deni's back and forth.

"Those are not symbols." Deni watched almost enjoying Stacy anticipate her next words. "They spell his name."

Tabatha, being used to going unseen, saw much was wrong with what was going on. She found being invisible had its advantages. "Sir," she chimed in, "we were only here to go over the layout with them." She waved her phone at Jason. "You still have two more stops before going over to the build in Seattle. We should be going."

Deni smiled in a way that got Jason's attention. "You didn't hear?" Her eyes were fixed on Jason. "That project has seen a bit of a delay. The wife of the architect leading the build has died under some very strange circumstances. Word is, they were going through a divorce, so of course, they're looking at him. There is no telling how long this will take them to clear up." Deni seemed to be working for a flinch in Jason's stare. "My colleague in Seattle told me the detective on the case is very good at what he does."

"Wish we had more time to talk," Benjamin said as Tabatha started ushering everyone towards the door. "Hope to see you next week. I still have several more questions for you."

"Why wait so long?" Jason's voice rode in on silk. It reminded Tabatha why he freaks her out. "She can join us tonight. Deni can celebrate with us."

"That's a great idea, Jason." Benjamin said as he walked past his driver who rushed to open the door for him.

"I think that could be fun." Deni brushed by Stacy as she walked over to Jason. "Text me the info." She stood there looking at Jason for a moment before turning to leave.

"Will he not need your mobile number to do that?" Tabatha asked.

"He has it," Deni said.

"You have her number?" Stacy looked at Jason. "Who is she? How true is what she said?"

"I truly couldn't tell you. There is something familiar in her eyes, but that green..." Jason thought back to something.

"Was it your grandmother that passed away when you had to go?" Stacy thought that would explain the change in him. "I thought your grandmother was still alive."

"She is. My father's mother is still alive, but…"

It was now clear to Stacy. "But your mother's mom isn't?"

"No, she's not," Jason confessed.

"If she truly knows you, why didn't she call us out?"

Stacy's voice pulled him back from thought. "I don't know that either."

"If she threatens to expose you, what then?"

"People disappear every day, never to be found again." Jason smiled at her.

"Will you get in the car already?"

Jason shook his head. "You go get pretty for tonight." He closed the door. As he started to walk away, he heard the window roll down.

"What are you going to do?"

"I don't know yet, but I may have a thing." He stopped and thought for a moment. "Invite the server girl to come out tonight and have her bring friends. Something to keep Benjamin's mind off asking questions about our employer."

RUFUS MONTGOMERY JR.

16

TONIGHT, IT FEELS LIKE I'M THE ONE BEING hunted. I wonder if I should give someone else a chance and just let her have… well, whatever it is she may want. It almost feels like the first time.

"Is this a new outfit?" Stacy asked as she adjusted my clothes. She does this every time we go anywhere she feels is important. Otherwise, she could care less what I'm wearing.

"Yes, indeed it is. Do you like?" I am dressed for the occasion. "It's a color I think I wear well."

"It does look good on you," Stacy said as she pulled my sleeves straight. I hate seeing her worried. She takes as good care of me as I do of her. In fact, she takes better care of me by far. Spending most of my life with only one person showing me I held a place in their heart is one thing, but now to have someone working as hard to show me they want a place in my life is a scary feeling for someone almost incapable of feelings.

"You look great yourself." I can't help but stare. "You're wearing it curly." I find it hard not to touch.

"How does a mind like yours get so distracted by curly hair? Are you going to be able to focus tonight, or do I need to go back up and change it?"

"No, I'll be fine." I hope. "Your dress looks great, and new as well. Was it expensive?"

"Oh, very."

Look at her showing off the parts of her I like the best.

"As well as you're paid, you can afford it. "

"Jason, you paid for it."

"Did I? I remember now why I don't like when you're upset. You get spendy." However, she's worth it with all the money she has made me over the years. I could never sell myself the way she can. Listening to her speak about me, I sometimes forget it is me she's talking about.

"Next time you'll know to let the man get creamed by the truck and stop making new friends. If this bitch keeps her shit up, come tomorrow we're going shoe shopping." What is she saying?

"What is this 'we' you speak of?"

She must be kidding. "We, as in I am taking you with me." Why is she looking at me like that?

"Why is it that you failed to mention this woman to me?" The hurt in her voice is apparent. Why does it bother me so much? Watching someone take his or her last breath doesn't bother me, but this could cause me to end a life or two this night. I'm pretty sure this isn't the best time to bring up Vicky.

The driver steps out of the car when he sees us approach the hotel doors. "When did you arrive, Mr. Miller?"

"I'm the assistant, so it's Jason, not Mr. Miller. However, she's Ms. Owens." I'm going to try my hand at being charming. "I got her, Steve. You just drive tonight."

Stacy paused for a moment. "How charming."

"Really?" Maybe I hit the mark this time.

"No, Jason, not really, but keep trying." She disappeared into the car.

"Maybe next time, Jason." Steve's words brought a chuckle with them.

"You don't have a steering wheel to wrap those oven mitts around? How fucking tall are you anyway? Where did I find you?" We both laugh and join Ms. Owens in the car.

"DID YOU TEXT HER THE ADDRESS FOR THE CLUB?" Stacy asks as she hopes I decided against it.

I know what she wants to hear me say, but I need to see how much this woman knows. "No, I did not text her the address."

"Good, then we won't have to worry about her answering anymore of Nat's questions about the artist." She sighed with relief.

"I took down her address and sent a car to drive her to the club." This needs to be as much under my control as I can make it. "I wanted to make sure she has no problem finding us."

"She seems to have no trouble finding you, but you decided to make it easier for her?"

RUFUS MONTGOMERY JR.

I don't often see Stacy like this. It's hard to tell if she is more mad or scared.

"How much of what she is saying is true? She even recognizes your signature. How is that she doesn't know you?"

"I don't know, Stacy. That's what I intend to find out tonight."

"But, how?" Her hand finds mine.

"Listen," I say, "you may have started out as a means to an end, but that is no longer the case. The things about me that I choose not to share with you are not things you want to know. I keep them from you to protect you, not because I don't trust you." Her face feels warm in my hands. It's a face I have killed for. "I don't want you sharing the burdens of my past, and some of my present. After the loss of my… well, you are now what tethers me to some form of humanity. You need to stay safe to keep many others the same. I go to great lengths to keep you that way."

Stacy is puzzled. "What are you talking about, Jason?"

She jumps when the door to the car swings open.

"We've arrived Miss Owens, Jason." Steve nods.

"Aren't you guys supposed to speak in rhyme?"

"Will you stop, before I ask him to step on you for my pleasure." Stacy says, as she emerges from the car with me close behind.

"Let me take one more look at you." She wants me to look my best. It almost feels like she knows how this night may end.

"It looks almost black." She holds my jacket up to her face. "Where did you find such a dark maroon?"

The thought of it all makes me smile. "It took some searching, but this is my color for such an occasion."

I take her hand ever so gently. "Shall we dance, Miss Owens?"

IT FEELS AS IF THE BEAT IS SQUEEZING MY HEART in synch. Stacy was right. In this light this shade looks black. Maybe this will be my new choice. The further into the crowd we stray, Stacy grips my hand tighter. "I have you." I have to almost put my mouth on her ear to have her hear me. I stop her before we reach Benjamin and Tabatha in the VIP section. With my arm around her waist, I pull her close and let the music take me. It's a few minutes before Stacy stops shaking and allow the music to take her as well. From the dance floor I can see that the server and her friends are enjoying Benjamin and his money. They are the distraction I was hoping they would be.

"We shouldn't keep our host waiting too long, plus your admirer should be here shortly." Stacy has her head on a swivel. "Last thing I want is for her to take the high ground."

I reclaim her hand and lead her to the VIP section. "Benjamin, it looks like you've met our friend." I take the glass he already has poured when he sees us walking to him. Benjamin is a man that thinks if you don't have a glass in your hand at a party, you are not having a good time. But this is going to have to go a little different than our normal nights out when we're in London to do business with his company.

"These girls are great." I can smell his last three drinks on his breath. "My guy is on his way here now with the good stuff."

When he says, "good stuff," and "his guy," he's talking about an Asian guy who seems to be able to get any drug you can think of. One night out with Benjamin, we watched this man cry himself to sleep like a baby right there on the sidewalk. Pretty sure he pissed himself.

"You didn't bring your friend out, Tab." If looks could kill. "After the last time I was lucky she stayed my friend. As for her coming, she doesn't even like being in London when you're here, much less in the same club as you. She still won't tell me what you two did back at her flat."

I smile at her and leave her to her own imagination.

"Look." Stacy presses her face against mine and points my head in the direction of Deni walking towards us. "I guess the car you sent managed to deliver her here. Now what?"

"You order your Black Russian, and I'll charm her into submission. Only leave with Steve tonight."

Stacy looks confused when I tell her that. I take another shot with Benjamin and leave to meet Deni.

"I'll take that Black Russian," Stacy says, "but if we have to count on your charm, we are really fucked."

RUFUS MONTGOMERY JR.

If she only knew the side of me whose charm had caused people to walk willingly to their death. I would rather her think me to have no charm than to know that side of me.

"Are you here to escort me?" Deni uses my shoulders to lift herself up to my height.

I shake my head but say nothing. Then I take her by her waist and lower her down, not letting her pull away from me. Her green eyes look oddly familiar.

"How long have you and Stacy worked for your artist?" Deni asks

"She's worked for him much longer than I, but when things started to grow, he brought me on as her assistant." The answer I give her has some truth in it. When she hears this, she smiles. It's a little unnerving, yet helpful.

"You've known one another for a while now?" If she means as Jason, then the answer she should hear is all my life. "We have worked together going on six years."

"What did you do before landing this job?" she asks.

"I traveled a lot," I say. She smells so good. "How about you? I am normally good with accents, but I can't quite place yours." She is very giving with her body while we dance.

"I have done a bit of traveling myself and other accents have found themselves intertwined with mine, I'm sure."

"How rude of me." I take her by the back of her head. Just to see how willing she is to give me control. She comes as close as I choose to bring her, looking as if she expects more. "I haven't even offered to buy you a drink." Instead of taking her to VIP, I lead her to the bar.

She keeps her eyes fixed on Benjamin and the others, but still follows me.

"Are we not joining your friends?" Deni asks when she realizes that I'm not taking her to VIP.

"Would you prefer me to want to share you with everyone up there?" I leave her to think on that as I order us drinks. Two Long Islands and a shot a piece. "Well?" I hand her the shot.

Her smile gives me her answer. "This works fine for me." We take the shot and start on the Long Islands. I order us one more shot and that seems to put her back into the dancing mood.

"What?" I see her lips moving but the music gets louder and keeps her words from making it to me.

"Are you two fucking?" Deni shouts over the music.

"Who would that be?" I know what she's asking, but I act like I don't, for good measure. This was a question she was going to have to ask.

"Stacy. Are you two fucking?" She looks over at Stacy.

At this point, I'm sure I wore the right color tonight. "No, Stacy and I are not fucking. Why do you ask?"

She ignores my question and has her own. "Can I fuck you then?"

"Looks to me that I gave you too much to drink too fast." I hold her by the chin and gaze into her eyes.

She looks to make sure we have Stacy's attention, and when she knows she does, she plants her lips on mine. Her tongue is wet and full, and her lips are soft and sweet. When she decides I've tasted enough, she peels away from me.

"Maybe I should make sure you get back to your hotel safe," I say.

"What about her?" She looks at Stacy as she wipes her lipstick off my lips.

Keeping my eyes locked on Deni, I say, "She is taken care of. We can go."

17

"ARE YOU NOT STAYING?" DENI ASKED JASON as she stepped out of her shoes.

"I delivered you safely to your hotel. I see no need to stay any longer." The hallway light shined over Jason's shoulders. "You know me, who I really am. We've established that. We've also established that you have no intention of telling anyone what you know. I see no reason to stay any longer."

"You're not the only one that can do what you do," she said as she rubbed her feet. "You saw me safe to the lobby." She licked the taste of him off her bottom lip. "Tell me, why are you standing there between what you should do and what you want to do?"

The click of the door sealing shut announced his decision. Jason's desire to know what Deni was doing here and how she knew so much, peaked. He took her in, trying to place her. In the past he had spent some time and great effort to disappear. Her explanation could be why she dies. "This is a nice room. What is it that you say you did?" Jason asked as he settled in across from her.

"Stop looking around trying to figure out how you would get my dead body out of here. Or even better, make it look like an accident." She smiled knowingly.

"What do you want? Even I have never played with my prey like this." His eyes narrowed. "If you know as much as you claim you know, this could be fun."

"As much fun as you had last night?" The words sounded almost like a song from her lips. "Do you find that she looks a lot like her? I find how you look at her reminiscent of how you used to look at Gwen."

"What the fuck did you say?" Jason looked down at her. "How do you know that name?"

"You truly left your past behind. Where did you go, Lyn? How do you not see me?" She wrapped her arms around his waist. "You've always looked at me, but never saw me. You never saw anything past Gwendolyn." She felt his body go limp at the sound of that name. "Yes, it's me. Do you see me now?" Her words were a whisper of things past.

"What?" He was unable to find the breath to give his word's life. "Why?" Her hands tightened around him, her hazel eyes pulling him out into the open. It was strange hearing her call him by that name. A name of a person he no longer was. "How did you find me?" His words finally found life. "Why even look for me?" He could feel his head floating. "You're not here," Jason muttered.

"But I am here, Lyn. You hear me, you smell me, and you can feel me. I am where I've always wanted to be. Where I should have been after…"

"Don't." She felt his body tense up.

"It's ok." She reassured him. "You are ready to hear it."

"Hear what?" His head swam. The words sounded as if someone else had spoken them. "What is it that you feel I am now ready to know?"

"Losing her should have brought us closer, but instead I lost you that day." Deni's chin pushed into Jason's chest, her eyes holding him in place. "Why would she do that to me? Why would she do that to you? Did any of it make any sense to you, or was who you were with her make you unable to see? I saw the you she did not—the you that's saved for special occasions."

"I thought she was happy. I thought we were happy," he whispered.

"We borrow happiness today with the hopes that tomorrow will pay the price."

Those words sounded familiar to him. "What is that from? I've heard that before."

"I would think so," Deni said as she removed something from her eyes. "Those were the last words until I heard you speak again at your grandmother's funeral. At Gwendolyn's funeral, I tried to find you after you spoke. I tried to find you, but you were nowhere to be found. I asked your mother, but like you said many times back then, she was of no help. Once again, I lost the chance."

"The chance to what?" he asked, now filled with real questions. "What did you want?"

"It's always been you. I wanted what she had, what you gave her. She had someone that would literally kill for her and didn't even know it. The way you looked at her was as if she was more important than the next breath you took. I wanted that. I saw you as you were and still loved you." Deni paused. He did indeed see the love in her hazel eyes that gazed up at him. "She was happy, and she would have never done that to us—not to you—Gwendolyn loved you too much. To her, there was no future without you in it. That's why I had to."

"You had to what, Deni?" Jason asked as her warm checks nestled against his hands.

"What I would have given to have you touch me like this back then. Why do you keep calling me that? Your eyes tell me you know who I am. With all you have done, you must have seen the signs. I thought when you said nothing and did nothing, I was right, and it would finally be us."

"There was a note. She left a note. It was her handwriting." He looked for sadness. He wanted to mourn her again.

"It was an assignment in her writing. She had to write how she would say goodbye to the people most important to her. It was how she would help us understand why she had to leave. Gwen was always such a great writer, and that had to have been one of her best pieces. That assignment gave me what I needed to make it look like she killed herself."

Jason felt her swallow deep. He pulled her to her feet, her eyes still fixed on him. He looked for anger. He wanted nothing more at that moment than to watch the life leave her eyes. He wanted his face to be the last she gazed upon before darkness took her. As sadness set in, anger abandoned him. Her lips on his quenched a thirst he did not know he had. Still on her toes, she reached down and worked his belt.

"You have to tell me this is real," she uttered what she could, pulling her lips away long enough to speak. "Who am I? You have to say it to make it real." She rubbed his side. "Call me by my name and make me real."

"Aubrey," he spoke her name like a prayer with such reverence.

She turned and led him to her room. Jason had the back of her dress pulled up and before Aubrey knew it, his hand came up from behind her, then his finger was inside her.

God." She felt the breath of that one word on her neck. He couldn't believe how wet she was. Jason's wrist was soaked from her inner thigh. She leaned her head against the door and could barely stand from her legs shaking. She was coming without delay. He put his arms around her to keep her up, but he kept his finger right where it was.

After she gathered herself, she swung the door open and pulled him in. By the look on her face, Jason could see who indeed she was. As she pulled him through the door by his belt, he had to watch his footing. As they made it to the bed, the only thing holding up his pants was her, although she did not do that for long. She dropped them and quickly went for his underwear. His dick was so hard it popped out like a Jack In The Box. His pants barely hit the floor before her warm wet tongue was on the shaft of his dick. She slowly moved it up and eased her mouth over the tip. Just the sound of it made his dick jump uncontrollably. Jason was not sure why, but she went into a frenzy and the gentle sucking turned into violent pulling and slurping. As much of him as she could fit in her mouth, she forced in. He stopped her before she could make him come. He had plans to fuck this woman. Not wanting her to pull it off, he used a little pressure to pull her up to him. Aubrey looked at Jason with hunger in her eyes. She wanted more. He turned her around and pushed her to the bed.

RUFUS MONTGOMERY JR.

Throwing her dress up onto her back, he to stepped out of his pants and underwear and kicked them behind him. Jason dropped to his knees and pulled off his shirt. As he kissed her inner thigh, he could tell they were still wet, and his kisses turned into licking. The sweet taste of it only made him want to drink from the source. He worked his way up and the closer he got, the more he could feel her shake. He stood up and looked down at her ass glistening from how wet her pussy was. He stepped forward slowly slipping into her making sure not to give her all just yet, but enough to touch that spot from earlier. He stood there as she rocked back and forth. He was there for her pleasure, and he let her use him. With her beautiful asshole looking up at him, he couldn't help but to play with it. He caressed it with his thumb, rubbing it in circles.

"God, it's so inviting."

She arched her back giving him an even better look. The more he played with it, the more he felt her tighten around his dick, and just like that, she was coming for the second time. Jason placed his right arm around her waist and braced himself. Now it was his turn to have fun. He put a little more of his finger in. She moaned. He pulled his dick out still dripping wet and rested it on her butt moving it slowly up and down. Jason pressed the head of his dick where his thumb was.

She whispered, "Please." She looked back at him.

He smiled. "Not this time." He pushed back into her throbbing pussy.

JASON LAID THERE. HIS DICK WAS STILL WET WITH the memory of what took place. As he listened to her breathe, he thought of himself as Lyn—a thing he had not done in years. In his mind, he had never stopped being him. Lyn was the one that bled onto the canvas. Jason was necessary to allow him to walk in the light yet be unseen. When he started to climb out of bed, she woke up.

"What are you doing?" Aubrey sat up in the bed.

His shoulder tensed up when he felt her lips. "I should leave." The words sounded more like a question.

RUFUS MONTGOMERY JR.

"There is no reason for you to go. Plus, you must be hungry. I know I am." The covers rolled free from her naked body.

"What are you doing?" He turned to see her inner thighs still glistened. She was still wet to the touch.

Aubrey's back arched. "See." She looked back. "You're not ready to leave yet. As you can tell, I'm not ready for you to leave either. I did just get you back."

Jason's hands tightened. "About that, how did you achieve it?"

Her muscle stiffened. "Achieve what?" Aubrey spread her legs ever so slightly trying to change the subject. Playfully, she traced his spine with her toes. "What did you want from room service?"

"No." His voice was soft but clear in its meaning. "How did you get me back? How did you find me? I went over everything and produced nothing. What are you even doing in London? I thought you moved back to Brazil."

"Lyn, that was over ten years ago. I see that you tracked me. I couldn't find you, but it seemed you knew where I was."

"Of course, I did. You were all I had left of her."

Those words were a sweet song to her ears.

"I didn't understand why you moved back to Brazil when your parents worked so hard to get you and your brother to the US. Why go back?"

She put the phone down. "After you left, people started to talk. They were saying that you and I must have had something going on that drove Gwen to do what she did."

"You mean, what *you* did." Jason corrected her.

"Yes, what I did." She agreed. "Being accused of betraying her bothered me more than being the one to take her life. What is wrong with us? You were always right about your parents. It took them over two years before they even called the Dean to see about you, and I'm sure it was only because of your grandmother."

"What do you mean?" The mention of his grandmother always brought him back from wherever it was he went. "What about mommy?"

"Yes, you did call her mommy, didn't you? Gwen would always say if she could only bottle the love you had for your grandmother and turn it into energy, she could solve all the world's problems. We watched you become human, just like that. This boy that was thought to feel little to nothing gushed with love for this little island woman. It was simply amazing. When you disappeared, that's where I thought you went, until she showed up weeks later looking for you. She was beside herself, and I saw her as my only chance to find you myself. I could see you leaving the world behind, but not her. Never her. So, I took her information and made sure to stay connected. As I was all you had left of Gwen, your grandmother was all I had left of you."

Fixed on her hazel eyes, Jason looked for every reason to let her live. "Mommy did mention how good you were to her and how you helped her cope with my absence. Mommy felt awful about not telling you when I contacted her."

Aubrey's toes responded to his hand. "I could tell when she started talking to you again. Your poor grandmother tried so hard to keep your secret and still ask all the questions you wanted answered. She would always reassure me that you would come back to us. Even after graduation and I moved back to Brazil, she and I stayed in contact. You were always our favorite subject. She even went as far as to ask why we did not get together. She is how I kept tabs on you."

Jason's mind took him back. "She told me you loved me," he whispered.

"What did you say?"

"She told me that you loved me," Jason repeated as if he questioned if it even happened.

"Your grandmother knew things before I could even tell her." Aubrey smiled when she thought back to some of their talks. "She would always refer to you as her king. I would sometime call her queen mother. I couldn't tell you how many times I heard the story of the day you were born. Pretty sure I can tell it as well as she could."

"I heard that story on every birthday right before she would cry." Jason became Lyn for that brief moment.

"As much as you meant to her, I knew she meant as much to you. When I stopped hearing from her as much as I used to, I knew something was wrong. Then I got the word that she had gotten sick. I knew where I could find you. However, before I could move things around to make it back stateside, she had died." She kicked at his hand when he didn't respond to her. He squeezed her foot. "At Gwen's funeral, I saw a part of you die, and what happened at your grandmother's funeral scared me."

"What happened? What scared you?" Jason asked as he thought back to that day.

"You. You scared me. More like what I saw you do." She could feel her blood go cold. "I watched you speak, and as you said your goodbyes to that beautiful woman, so did you kill what was left of Lyn. I watched Jason walk out of that church. When they lowered her into the ground, they unknowingly put Lyn in the ground as well."

He felt like he couldn't catch his breath when he heard her speak those words.

"With her, you were truly human. Now, what we see is you simply playing human." Aubrey noticed she had lost Lyn. Or was it Jason she lost? "Who are you when you do it?" Aubrey asked.

"When I do what?" The light shined on his face.

"When you kill. Who are you when you do that?" she asked as she pushed her chin down onto the covers.

"That answer only matters to those who see that face at the end. I don't see why that should matter to the living." He put his phone away.

"Why do you care so much about her?"

"Excuse me?"

"Stacy. Why do you care so much about her? Who is she to you?" Aubrey's voice sounded peppered.

"My assistant. She keeps the eyes off me and makes it possible for both Lyn and Jason to exist." He looked for his other phone.

"Does she know?" Aubrey sounded afraid of the answer.

"I truly do not know what she does or doesn't know at this point," Jason said as he made a small opening in the curtains. The city was still awake. "All I know is I'm glad she did not end up dead."

"She still shows up in your paintings. Did you know that?" Aubrey said, knowing the risk in her words. "That's partly how I found you again. I gave up trying to get your grandmother to break and tell me how to find you. She would have made a great spy. That woman knew how to avoid questions. Especially when it came to your whereabouts. I stopped asking and was just happy she hinted that she knew you were doing ok. When I was finally ready to face that I may never see you again, I saw you on the wall of one of my clients. Those blue flames gave you up. You did always want to see the world burn."

Jason titled his head back and breathed in and out, trying to calm the storm that was now brewing inside of him.

"At first, I thought there could be no way this was your work, but then I saw the scribble you call a signature. When my client told me how he obtained your painting, I started looking for more of your work. Everyone that had one of your works had a similar story on how they purchased the piece. The artist that everyone wanted on their wall, but no one had ever seen. I thought it funny that you always hated to show your paintings, and only painted to get away from the numbers. Now, here was your work more sought after by collectors."

"I know it made me laugh," Jason said. "It became all I wanted to do. In no way did I plan for it to come to this. It all happened so fast. Stacy helped me hide in plain sight. I left that day as Lyn but came back five years later as Jason Miller. My grandmother was the only one I visited, and she kept my secret. I was there with her on some occasions when you would call.

Every time I heard her tell you the story of the day I was born, I knew it was her way of trying to tell you I was there with her." The pillow Aubrey threw almost pushed his head into the window. "She looked almost as mad as you look right now every time, she had to lie to you about me." He picked up the pillow. "Stacy was never supposed to leave Italy alive. She was there to let me be in a room with my paintings and a buyer for the first time. I had to see if it could be done."

"So, why is she still alive? What happened?" Aubrey couldn't hide the disappointment in her voice.

Jason's eyes went dead for a moment. "Someone else died in her place when she showed her value, and now, here we are." He examined Aubrey's face. "Why did you go through so much trouble to look different? I loved your red hair and those little cheerleader shorts you used to wear. Guys in class wouldn't shut up about you."

"I didn't want to risk you seeing me coming. You have to understand—I didn't know if you even wanted to see me. Moreover, I was unsure if you figured out what I had done, and if I would have the opportunity to explain myself before you decided to kill me. I had to see what death now meant to you."

"When did you decide I would not kill you as soon as I knew who you were?"

"When I saw you save that man from getting nailed by that truck. It would have been so easy for you to have let him die, but you saved him." She tried to find his plans for her in his eyes. Did she still even know this man in front of her? "When you did not recognize me when I spoke to you, I saw my chance."

Being the planner he was, he still could not see where he left the opening. "How did you find me in London? Stacy didn't even know we would be here until I sent her traveling information. Only then did she know we would be working with Benjamin again. Nothing was putting me in London until I stepped on to the plane bringing me here."

"I didn't meet you here, I followed you here," she said. "I was in Seattle when you were."

"But how did you know I…" Jason stopped when he heard his words. He saw how much like him she truly was at that moment. Now he knew what he was looking at.

"By the look in your eyes, Lyn, you've worked it out. Your honor made you the best son you could be to a woman that cared little for you. We watched you work so hard to make proud a father that didn't see you. Love brought you to mommy's funeral, but I knew honor and obligation would bring you to your uncle's," Aubrey explained.

Jason laughed. "You killed him." His voice filled with an odd glee. "Here I was thinking his wife had something to do with it." He licked his lips still able to taste Aubrey on them.

"Seeing you with your other grandmother made me sad to see how you tried to find something with her that you lost when your other grandmother died. Where you received true love from mommy, your father's mother simply played at being something to you. She was what you needed at that time to look human to those who looked on."

"How much did you see in Seattle, Aubrey?" Things started to become clear to him. "The woman in the bar. Did you have anything to do with her?"

"Yes. She was a hooker I paid to keep an eye on you. I couldn't risk doing it myself. I wasn't ready to approach you yet. I still did not know who you became yet, so I stayed out of sight." She sounded almost apologetic.

RUFUS MONTGOMERY JR.

Jason looked at her waiting to hear what more she may have seen.

"All the time I spent admiring your paintings, they couldn't compare to watching you at your true art. I saw that your skills with a paintbrush were surpassed with your skills at death."

"And now, here we are," Jason said bringing Aubrey's story to an end.

"Yes Lyn, here we are." Her legs dangled off the bed. She could feel his eyes on the back of her head.

As his hands crossed and she felt the towel tightened around her throat she could not help but smile. When her hand finally made it up her thighs and her finger found her clit, Jason could feel her body relax. His stiff cock on the small of her back made it hard to stop himself. The harder he squeezed the wetter she became. The two fingers that slid into her pussy faced no resistance. As she pushed in and out of herself, she took in less and less air. Feeling herself coming, she let go of the world around her and welcomed in the thought of death. His gentle kiss on the top of her head and the air rushing back into her lungs caused her to come even harder the second time. Jason lowered her shaking body to the bed.

He kissed her quivering lips. "I think I'm ready for that room service." He reclaimed his towel and made his way to the bathroom. "Could you order me a…"

Aubrey out of breath interrupted "I know."

"So be it," he replied.

Aubrey lay there for a moment, putting her thoughts back together before lifting the phone. "Is this room service?" she asked, still a little out of breath. "Good, I would like to order a Ruben with heavy pickles on the side. How's your flatbread pizza? Ok, I will take one of those." She listened as they repeated it all back to her. "Wait, before I forget." She stopped him before he could finish. "I would also like a cheesecake and oatmeal raisin cookies please." A smile crept onto her lips.

MORE BOOKS BY THE AUTHOR

The Heart of the Sword
The Heart of the Sword II: His World Ablaze

www.ingramcontent.com/pod-product-compliance
Lightning Source LLC
Chambersburg PA
CBHW020418010526
44118CB00010B/302